Special Women, Special Leaders

Studies in the
Postmodern Theory of Education

Joe L. Kincheloe and Shirley R. Steinberg
General Editors

Vol. 284

PETER LANG
New York • Washington, D.C./Baltimore • Bern
Frankfurt am Main • Berlin • Brussels • Vienna • Oxford

Special Women, Special Leaders

Special Educators and the Challenge of Leadership

Marsha H. Lupi and Suzanne M. Martin

EDITORS

PETER LANG
New York • Washington, D.C./Baltimore • Bern
Frankfurt am Main • Berlin • Brussels • Vienna • Oxford

Library of Congress Cataloging-in-Publication Data

Special women, special leaders: special educators and the challenge
of leadership / edited by Marsha H. Lupi and Suzanne M. Martin.
p. cm. — (Counterpoints: studies in the postmodern theory of education; vol. 284)
Includes bibliographical references.
1. Women—Education (Higher)—United States.
2. Educational leadership—United States. 3. Women college administrators—
United States. I. Lupi, Marsha H. II. Martin, Suzanne M.
III. Series: Counterpoints (New York, N.Y.); v. 284.
LC1756.S64   378.1′11′082—dc22   2005012820
ISBN 0-8204-7264-6
ISSN 1058-1634

Bibliographic information published by **Die Deutsche Bibliothek**.
Die Deutsche Bibliothek lists this publication in the "Deutsche
Nationalbibliografie"; detailed bibliographic data is available
on the Internet at http://dnb.ddb.de/.

Cover design by Lisa Barfield

The paper in this book meets the guidelines for permanence and durability
of the Committee on Production Guidelines for Book Longevity
of the Council of Library Resources.

This book is dedicated to all women who have devoted their lives to the education of students with disabilities and those who teach them, with a special tribute to our mothers, Mary Geraldine Martin and Beverly Herman and to Alexis Rose Lupi, a loving daughter, for whom the leadership path lies ahead.

Table of Contents

Foreword

Barbara P. Sirvis

The Road Not Taken

TWO roads diverged in a yellow wood,
And sorry I could not travel both
And be one traveler, long I stood
And looked down one as far as I could
To where it bent in the undergrowth;

Then took the other, as just as fair,
And having perhaps the better claim,
Because it was grassy and wanted wear;
Though as for that, the passing there
Had worn them really about the same,

And both that morning equally lay
In leaves no step had trodden black.
Oh, I kept the first for another day!
Yet knowing how way leads to way,
I doubted if I should ever come back.

I shall be telling this with a sigh
Somewhere ages and ages hence:
Two roads diverged in a wood, and I—
I took the one less traveled by,
And that has made all the difference.

—Robert Frost (1874-1963)

It's all about the journey, the individual choices with which we are all faced throughout our lives. Our paths contain numerous roads that diverge in the woods of our personal and professional lives. In special education, some choose to be dedicated classroom teachers who daily provide education, motivation and nurturance for children and youth with disabilities. Others are drawn, often for some unknown or unidentifiable reason or due to an unexpected opportunity, to leadership roles—in a school building, a school district, higher education, government agencies and/or in professional organizations.

This book is the first attempt to capture the unique experiences and journeys to leadership by women in special education. The editors celebrate the individual and collective journeys of the contributors and recognize their examples of important roles and the contributions of women in leadership roles in special education. The challenges faced by the women who share their experiences in this book provide unique examples of divergent paths to leadership and the challenges faced in the process.

When Ann Morrison (1990) first wrote of the proverbial "glass ceiling," she examined only the corporate sector. Since that work, the "glass ceiling" has become a regular part of the vernacular in addressing the leadership challenges faced daily by women in a variety of sectors. In education, the glass ceiling was "cracked" when women first achieved the role of building principal. Traditionally, women provided their leadership within the classroom where they fulfilled the important role of guiding the academic and social development of young people. A woman superintendent was a rarity until the last quarter of the twentieth century.

In higher education, similar situations occurred as women gradually were admitted to the ranks of faculty but not to administrative positions. Even now, although women are the gender majority in the overall population and among college students, women represent less than 40 percent of faculty and slightly more than 20 percent of presidential positions (American Council on Education, 2004).

Whether male or female, the rise of special educators to senior administrative positions is relatively recent. Before the advent of "mainstreaming," special educators worked in special schools, hospitals and institutions where they rarely interacted with their general education colleagues. Advancement and leadership opportunities were limited to these isolated environments. As special education services moved to more inclusive environments, opportunities began to emerge for special educators to assume levels of leadership beyond the specialized setting. Seemingly, there was a parallel with the history of leadership development in education as men in special education received early promotions to the first administrative openings in schools after "mainstreaming." A similar parallel existed in higher education as men rather than women in higher education more often became department chairs and then became deans. To this author's knowledge, only two individuals (one male and one female) with special education backgrounds have risen to the presidency of a higher education institution. Marsha H. Lupi and Suzanne M. Martin, both of whom have held multiple leadership roles, asked several of their colleagues to provide individual perspectives on the challenges they each and all faced in the evolution of their leadership roles. In the opening chapter, they create the framework and overall perspective for the book and examine numerous factors—spouses, partners, children, opportunities and finances—that may impact the rise to leadership positions. While much of the focus is on higher education, the discussion of women's leadership styles has applicability across many venues. They look at the "special education connection" to leadership and the skills acquired in the profession that can become fundamental to fostering positive change.

"Leadership is never a solo endeavor. The ideas and actions of leaders do not materialize in a vacuum. In fact, leadership is the product of a relationship between people, each contributing experience, insight and expertise to create a whole that is greater than the sum of its parts" (Lagemann, 2002, p.3). Sharon Cramer provides a framework for the collaboration skills that assist women in leadership. While the roles may vary among sectors, the demands and strategies cross those boundaries. Cramer suggests "keys" to successful collaboration that provide a framework for individual consideration of style and leadership roles.

Paths to leadership often take unusual turns, or unexpected challenges provide opportunities for leadership. Consider the many parents who were advocates for their children in the early days of "mainstreaming," long before we developed to the current concept of inclusion. Today parents continue to play a vital role in advocacy roles for their own and others' children with disabilities. In their chapter, Susan Donavan and Mary Senne write eloquently of the challenges faced by parents and their choices to provide leadership as a result of their experiences. As "mother/leaders," their insight should be helpful for advocates, leaders and other parents.

The role of the executive director of a professional organization is to provide leadership "behind the scenes," and, as a colleague once said to me of her role as an association executive, "to make the president look good." It is a role with many demands for day-to-day operational leadership and organizational advocacy within policies created by volunteer leaders in the association. Nancy

D. Safer, former Executive Director of the Council for Exceptional Children (CEC) and the first woman to hold that position, discusses the challenges of association leadership, noting that women more often have the skills for—and yet less often are found in—the role of association executive. She explores the realities and dilemmas that create a situation where it is unlikely that women will achieve their leadership potential in associations.

Founded by Elizabeth E. Farrell at Teachers College, Columbia University in 1922, The Council for Exceptional Children has become the lead advocate and "voice" for special education services and personnel. Farrell served as president until 1926, after which the majority of presidents were men. It is interesting to note that between 1922 and 1970, only ten women served as president while twenty-nine men held the lead office. A noticeable change occurred beginning in 1971; since then, fifteen women and seventeen men have held the presidential role. Diane Johnson, Pamela Gillet and Linda Marsal were among those fifteen women, and write of their own more recent experiences providing leadership to CEC through some challenging times for the association and for special education. All of the authors held leadership roles within their respective school districts at the time of their election, and they all agree that there is a parallel in the leadership skills required in the schools and required of the leader of the largest advocacy organization for special education students and professionals.

"The glass ceiling is firmly intact in academe at the start of the twenty-first century" (Berryman-Fink, LeMaster & Nelson, 2003, p.59). Several of the authors are among those women in special education who are serving in leadership roles in higher education and, as a result, are breaking the "glass ceiling" in the academy. In their respective chapters, Deborah A. Shanley, and Kathleen McSorley and LeeAnn Truesdell examine higher education leadership opportunities from the differing perspectives of line and staff positions. The demands, expectations, and responsibilities are no less important and yet quite different. Assistant and Associate Deans often face more of the "real" day-to-day operational work that affects the success of a division within the university. The Dean is more likely to have to take the "fire" of the unique and demanding political environment that is found at the institutional level. The authors note that those in staff positions are expected to provide leadership for program development and creation of new initiatives. To be successful requires finely honed facilitation skills because Assistant and Associate Deans do not have the budgetary control that could create natural incentives. At the same time, the Dean more often has to make—or take responsibility for—the decisions that will make someone unhappy when "win-win" is not possible.

Leadership in schools, higher education, and even professional associations provides for opportunities for direct impact on the classroom environment for students with disabilities. Whether preparing teachers for those classrooms, advocating for appropriate policies or providing district-based leadership, none of these environments can match the bureaucracy of a federal governmental agency. Suzanne M. Martin and Jane M. Williams address first the unique, usually personal pathways that led them to civil service. They examine the characteristics that sometimes force women to accept change as a challenge rather than a barrier to professional growth. They provide insight into how one can create voice within the bureaucracy to impact "the system." Beyond the choice to assume a government position, they also explore the "moral compasses" that allowed them to stay focused and productive in the large and potentially overwhelming morass of the U.S. Department of Education.

Vivian I. Correa and Patricia Alvarez McHatton explore the need to enhance faculty diversity at colleges and universities. Even as these institutions seek to diversify their student body, students do not necessarily find familiar faces and backgrounds with whom to identify in their own development. While special education classrooms continue to have a diverse population, higher education personnel who prepare teachers for the students of today and tomorrow do not reflect the diversity found in the classroom. While this entire text focuses on the issue of gender, there is a major challenge in finding faculty who represent culturally and linguistically different backgrounds as well as those who excel in the face of their own disabilities. They present ideas for the creation of networks to expand diverse representation in higher education.

Virtually all of the authors discuss the challenge of balancing the personal and professional aspects of their lives. Wendy W. Murawski, Pokey Stanford, Nancy Sileo and Lisa Dieker look at the conflicting demands faced by women faculty in the academic environment. They share candidly their own situations and then the strategies they use to attempt to find the balance in their lives without forsaking the joys and challenges of both their personal and professional lives.

All the authors share their own personal and professional "stories," and readers will find those situations and reflections that resonate most for them. Ultimately, the words of Cokie Roberts in her insightful historical book *Founding Mothers* have to ring true as we read and consider each chapter: "They did— with great hardship, courage, pluck, prayerfulness, sadness, joy, energy and humor—what women do. They put one foot in front of the other in remarkable circumstances. They carried on" (2004, p. xx). This book celebrates and honors all women in special education who in carrying on often took the road less traveled. Indeed, it often made all the difference for people with disabilities and others whose lives these authors touched.

References

American Council on Education (2004). *The American College President*, 2002 edition. Washington, DC: American Council on Education.

Berryman-Fink, C., B. J. LeMaster, & K. A. Nelson (2003). The Women's Leadership Program: A Case Study. *Liberal Education*, 89 (1), 59-63.

Lagemann, E. C. (2002). *Harvard Graduate School of Education, 2001-2002 Annual Report*. Cambridge, MA: Harvard University.

Roberts, C. (2004). *Founding Mothers: The Women Who Raised Our Nation*. New York: HarperCollins.

Preface

This book is written with great respect for the women we have met in our lives who continually amaze us by their leadership skills. One thing we know for sure—it is not always easy to have a professional life while trying to manage a personal life. Creating a balance between leadership and the important roles women play as mothers, daughters, sisters, wives, partners and friends is not always easy. However, we have seen it done day after day, time after time, by women who have accepted the role of leadership in schools, universities, agencies and professional organizations. The juggling of carpools, caring for elderly parents and making sure cupcakes are bought for a birthday party are only a few of life's activities that working women are still largely responsible for and that they perform regularly despite assuming demanding and challenging careers.

The chapters in this book are written by women who have accepted the challenge and responsibility of leadership in the fields of special education and higher education. For those authors teaching and leading in colleges and universities, careers are continually shaped and formed by a common set of internal and external forces. Among the key challenges for academic women are "publish or perish," teaching overloads, extensive field supervision for those in schools or colleges of education, and other related pursuits necessary for tenure and promotion in the university. Our authors who have dedicated their lives to public schools have experienced the stresses and challenges of the profession as they persistently work with students with disabilities and their families. This work is done on a daily basis in school systems that are continually undergoing changes driven by new and emerging education laws and certification requirements. The remaining chapter authors have chosen or experienced a leadership pathway through professional organizations and government agencies. They have written about the specific challenges they have faced in leadership roles that involved them with large numbers of people and important legislation.

We are privileged to personally know the authors in this book, and feel confident they have accurately shared their stories, insight and recommendations on the challenges of leadership postmodern women face in the twenty-first century. We thank them for their wisdom, time, energy and devotion to preparing others to lead after them.

Marsha H. Lupi
Suzanne M. Martin

CHAPTER ONE

Women Leaders in Higher Education and the Special Education Connection

MARSHA H. LUPI AND SUZANNE M. MARTIN

Transformational leadership feels right to women because it is not asking anything that they haven't done"

—*Jacquelyn M. (2003)*

The characteristics, skills and dispositions of effective leaders in any field need to be comprehensive and varied. The range and complexity of issues facing higher education today are particularly daunting. Effective leaders in higher education must have the ability to recognize and define challenges and opportunities continuously. They must be able to collaborate with a broad range of stakeholders to develop appropriate strategies to ameliorate the weaknesses and build on the strengths of existing programs, practices and policies. Higher education leaders must lead the effort to provide support structures that will help to motivate and reward students, faculty and staff and they must know how to develop public understanding and support for the work of their institution.

No single mold for producing leaders who will be able to accomplish all of the above exists. Some leaders will be stronger in some dispositions and skills than in others. Some will be better leaders in some situations than in others. Some will operate most effectively when they are personally heading every effort while others will be most effective while delegating leadership roles more broadly. An effective leader does not have to have every skill and disposition or be able to do everything personally. Rather, an effective leader needs to know what skills and dispositions are needed and how to bring human and other resources to the table to get the job defined clearly and done well.

There is considerable literature that speaks to the dimensions of effective leadership and, to a lesser extent, to the differences that may exist between women and men in exhibiting these dimensions. This literature does not suggest that any particular characteristic, skill or disposition is the sole province of females or males but that, due to differences in experiences, socialization, opportunities or other factors, there are likely to be differences in how women and men develop and demonstrate their leadership styles. Females can and do adopt leadership styles traditionally associated with males, and the converse is also true. However, we believe it is important and instructive to examine the nature and genesis of general differences in male and female leadership styles and to use that knowledge in considering how to address more specific issues relating to understanding and developing female leaders in higher education.

This chapter will seek to provide a framework for understanding and identifying the particular leadership styles of women, especially in colleges and universities; contrast various leadership styles as they relate to gender; examine the positive nature of transformational leadership; review pathways to leadership and the factors that influence them; and explore what we believe are valuable connections between being a special educator and being an effective leader.

Leadership Styles of Women and Men

Eagly, Wood and Diekman (2000) have separated traditional leadership styles for women and men into two general categories: Agnetic (Male) and Communal (Female). Women as communal leaders are oriented toward interpersonal relationships and are more employee centered, more willing to share information and decision making. Women are more likely to demonstrate transformational leadership (Eagly & Johannesen-Schmidt, 2001). They often appear to view job performance as assisting subordinates to transform their own self-interest into the interest of the group, thereby maintaining concern for a broader goal. Women ascribe their power to personal characteristics like charisma, interpersonal skills, hard work or personal contacts rather than to organizational status (Rosener, 1990).

Men have often been observed to demonstrate agnetic leadership, which is characterized by problem-focused, competitive, ambitious and assertive behavior that is best defined as job centered, with a major concern on performance of employees (Eagly, Wood & Diekman, 2000). They are often more task-oriented and more autocratic and directive than women. Bass, as cited in Oyinlade, Gellhaus and Darboe (2003 reports that men exhibit transactional leadership. Trans-actional leadership stresses "the leader's ability to clarify organizational goals, roles and the requirement of tasks" (Oyinlade, Gellhaus & Darboe, 2003, p. 390). Men are more likely to use power that comes from their place in the organizational hierarchy and formal authority than are women leaders.

Women, according to Orman (2004) also exhibit "Generative leadership". They practice what the psychologist Erik Eriksen has coined as "generativity," or the "outward-turned behavior to nurture the next generation" (p. 5). In Erik-sen's model, generativity is the seventh of eight stages of psychosocial devel-opment and is the task of middle adulthood (ages 40-65). Most women leaders, including those in a study done by Dr. Orman on women academic deans and associate deans, fit this age range. They exhibit "Interactive Leadership" (Rose-ner, 1990) by encouraging participation and aiming for an enhanced feeling of self worth in the lives of their employees. As "generative leaders," women cre-ate a work culture that values people (Jablonski as cited in Orman, 2004). Their leadership styles often incorporate shared or collective decision making, inclu-sion of a wide range of viewpoints, public rather than private problem solving, legitimization of persons as well as groups and units within an organization, and open communication (Book, 2000; Johnson, 1993). Johnson states that "Ad-ministrators who view themselves as practicing feminist processes are seldom concerned with aggrandizing power, and are rarely concerned about establishing strong personal claims to 'authorship' for ideas and innovations" (p. 13).

At the 2004 Women's Breakfast at the 56th annual conference of the American Association of Colleges of Education, the keynote speaker, Dr. Mary Catherine Bateson, made reference to women as "Peripheral Visionaries." One interpretation of this term is that women not only have a clear vision of what is ahead of them, but they also are able to effectively sense that which surrounds them. This vision is an invaluable skill, one that perhaps has its most basic and prehistoric origins in the more traditional role of women as mothers and pro-tectors of children from wild animals and any other dangerous situation. Rose-ner (1990) states that survival tactics come easily to women given the challenges associated with their socialization and status over centuries and in a variety of cultures. Sarah Gibbard Cook (2004) writes that instead of "fight or flight," women's response is to "tend and befriend," and in times of great stress they will come to the aid of each other, taking care of children and others in need.

Implications for Women as Leaders in Higher Education

We believe that the dispositions and characteristics of women described above carry with them great significance for effective, empathetic and assertive leadership for postmodern women leaders in higher education. We also believe that a woman leader will probably need a combination of male and female leadership traits to be effective. However, without traits such as those described in the literature as typical to women, it would be very difficult to develop the trust that is needed between a leader and those she is assigned to lead. As leaders, we often are "pushed" to be more efficient—but efficiency and meeting the needs of people are not always compatible. As Covey, Merrill and Merrill (1994) ask, "Have you ever tried to be efficient with your spouse or your teenager or an employee on an emotional jugular issue? How did it go? Don't bother me now, son. Just take your emotional broken and bleeding self somewhere else for a few minutes while I finish my 'to do' item" (p. 26). Building trust takes time. Women as highly collaborative leaders are likely to take that time.

In addition, a leader who works to create and maintain a community of supporters will actively, through their daily work, be more likely to be successful in transforming the vision of the leader and of the organization into reality. Pearce (2001) discusses the hard work required to do this as being that of a "soft manager." He elaborates by saying that "soft management does not mean weak management. It means candor, openness and vulnerability, but it also means hard choices and responsible follow up." (p. 89). Women in leadership roles in higher education often have great need for and are adept at exhibiting these "soft" qualities.

Human beings have four basic needs to be fulfilled: physical, social, mental and spiritual. Relationships built on trust value these needs and see them as very important. Achieving balance among these four needs is challenging, but if the balance does not occur, quality of life of the individual and, ultimately, the organization will suffer. The integration of these needs can lead to an inner synergy that will give passion, vision and spirit to life (Covey et al., 1994). Our review of the literature strongly supports the notion that women leaders, particularly those with special education backgrounds, usually have a "passion within" that allows that inner synergy to shine.

Finally, leadership involves change and change is rarely easy. We know that early adopters of innovations often only comprise 5 percent to 10 percent of the total group. Change is often related to a leader's style and attitude toward it. In their seminal work, Tannenbaum and Schmidt (1957) found a variety of styles within a set of extremes, from the leader making the decision and announcing it to the leader, allowing the group to make the decision within a very broad set of defined limits. Tucker (1984) in his book, *Chairing the Academic Department*, states that based on the continuum of leadership style, as outlined in Tannenbaum and Schmidt, three criteria are involved in the degree to which faculty become involved in change. They are expertise, acceptance and time. These criteria will vary in importance according to circumstance. A leader must consider to what degree and at what points, in various circumstances, members of the group need to be involved in decision making. Hefferlin (1972) finds that few institutions exhibit spontaneous change. "In most social groups, a creative tension exists between forces that operate to bring about change and forces that operate to resist change" (Tucker, 1984, p. 103). Women who possess strong collaboration skills and the ability to listen and accept ideas, who have expertise in problem-solving and who pursue change with full consideration of the context of beliefs and values of the group are more likely to be successful change agents. Many of the women we have come to see as our role models have been very effective change agents. They have been able to remain focused on necessary outcomes, to clearly articulate their vision for the organization and implement change with honesty and integrity. These leaders have the ability to motivate a group initially, maintain the momentum needed to move a group forward, and reward the people involved in the process. As we will discuss later in greater detail, it is noteworthy that these skills and dispositions are often found among special educators.

The Paths We Take

As female children and youth, most likely there were women whom we looked up to and admired. We may not have been able to articulate exactly what it was about the person, but we knew that by being in their company we could achieve something important and feel safe in the process. It may have been a teacher, youth counselor, next-door neighbor, our mothers or other family members. These women had a certain "charisma," that undefinable, exciting quality that motivated us to begin our own journeys toward becoming productive and fulfilled women and future leaders. We wanted to follow their example for many reasons but primarily because they supported us and facilitated our development rather than criticized or dictated what our actions should be. They became our role models for human behavior and leadership; women who managed to effectively blend the responsibilities of leadership with the personal demands of home and family and the importance of the individual.

As we have matured and moved out into the world and into our respective careers, we have encountered even more women who have demonstrated the art and science of effective leadership. We have come to recognize that the pathways they take to leadership are diverse and complex and are contingent on many factors such as spouses/partners, children, status differentials and financial considerations. While these factors are also important in determining male pathways to leadership, females often have had to traverse these pathways via different and more circuitous routes than males.

Numerous pathways to becoming a leader exist. These pathways can be considered *linear*, such as ascending a career ladder, *branching*, like a tree sprouting different branches at times of different needs, and/or born from partners and places, such as following a spouse to a new position or moving somewhere based solely on job availability (Women in Higher Education, 2002). Women who move into positions of leadership in institutions of higher education may take any of these various paths. Lupi (2004), in her study of women with backgrounds in special education who currently are in deanship positions, found that several of the study participants began their careers in higher education leadership while holding positions as assistant professors.

Several remarked they were "reluctant administrators" who had taken administrative positions in the university because of their senses of loyalty to the university and with the belief that if they did not take the position, no one else would and an important role in working toward improvement would not be filled. These women reported a direct connection between their preparation as special educators and their decisions to accept a leadership position for the overall good of their peers. Another group in the study found they were in their positions due to a spousal move. Gilda Munson (2004) used an interesting term when she refers to herself as the "trailing spouse," stating that she followed her heart over her head. She left a three-year position at an elite university to move with her husband to his first tenure-earning position. She has since obtained a position as assistant professor at a university near her husband's job. Participants in Lupi's study who moved to follow their spouses stated that they had finished their graduate work due to the move and now were on the academic pathway that many consider linear.

For many other women, the pathways they took to a leadership role in higher education seem circuitous at best. Typical steps along the way have included branching experiences such as holding public school teaching positions, volunteering for leadership positions in the community, adapting their career progress due to family, financial or other exigencies, moving to take new positions and thus facing continuing change, leaving the world of work to raise children, and returning to higher education at later points in their careers to assume varying levels of leadership. The wealth and variety of skills and dispositions these women can transfer from these experiences to the leadership positions they hold can be incredibly valuable to institutions of higher education. Many of the issues involved in preparing students well and leading faculty and staff in today's higher education institutions are related to the same cross-section of circumstances and experiences. While many of the women who choose this branching pathway are often met with tenure committees who believe in "the baby or the book", they have chosen to attempt balancing their love for their work with their love for their families. The Allen Group, an employee assistance program, sees these women like most working parents as wearing many hats and needing to use every available resource to maintain their balance (The Allen Group, 2004).

Dr. Patricia Bowie Orman has been studying women in academic dean positions since 2001. At the American Educational Research Association meeting in 2004, she stated that women academic deans usually do not follow the traditional pathway to leadership model. She found these women to have different patterns, motives and prior experiences yet this diverse group shared a common leadership style—nurturing. When Orman interviewed deans and associate deans, she found recurring themes. The women interviewed had not planned careers in academic leadership; they led and made decisions collaboratively; they regarded power as negative; and, most did not aspire to higher levels of administration. Many of these women saw their jobs as temporary and as their duty to the college. The associate deans interviewed stated they were surprised that their role did not prepare them to be a dean. They felt constrained by grunt work, communication issues and invisibility. Due to the lack of advancement opportunities they often did not move up, they moved out.

Women often are faced with institutional status barriers to their advancement as well. A recent report from the Harvard Graduate School of Education indicates that major differences in the treatment of men and women in the academic workplace exist. Cathy Trower (2001), the study's primary author, found that large research universities were not as inviting or as supportive of women in research roles as they were of men in similar roles. According to Trower's study, women were significantly less satisfied than men in their roles as researchers. The women were particularly unhappy about the university expectation of their productivity and felt that many universities still adhere to "a father knows best" attitude when it comes to women climbing the promotion and tenure ladder. It should be no surprise that women many times seek other career paths in higher education, including administration, in the face of such obstacles. The study encourages research institutions to provide stronger mentoring programs, train people to be department chairpersons and create more family-friendly policies.

The Support We Need

Given the difficulty and variety of the career paths women leaders in higher education often take, it is essential that appropriate and adequate support be available at many points along the way. Dean's (2004) National Study of Women Chief Academic Officers found that the most frequently cited professional activities that seemed to accelerate movement for women leaders were attendance at leadership development programs, receiving mentoring, having external visibility and planning their careers. Of the 375 respondents, 81 percent had participated in one to six leadership programs with several of these identified as being particularly well formulated and of much practical assistance to career advancement. An excellent example of a leadership-training program for women is the Higher Education Resource Services (HERS) Summer Institute at Bryn Mawr. It offers women faculty and administrators intensive training in education management and governance of colleges and universities. The curriculum prepares participants to work with issues currently facing higher education, with emphasis on the growing diversity of the student body and the work force. HERS is designed to improve the status and opportunities of women in academe, especially those in the mid levels of administration (e.g., associate dean). The Institute is committed to the development of a professional network of skilled women administrators ready to be mutually supportive and to work cooperatively to enlarge the professional opportunities for women in higher education. HERS curriculum includes instructional units on Academic Environment (e.g., undergraduate learning and teaching, diversity issues such as recruiting minority faculty and students), External Environment (e.g., financial conditions impacting public and private colleges, external demands for accountability at the state and national levels), Institutional Environment (e.g., financial and accounting processes; budgeting techniques and politics) and Professional Development (e.g., addresses the needs of the individual woman as she functions within the institutional context, giving special attention to leadership skills, public speaking and self-presentation as well as balancing one's life). The session is supplemented each year by an informal curriculum tailored to the special interests identified by that summer's class. The faculty of HERS comes from diverse sectors of North American higher education including professional associations, foundations, government agencies and universities. As Dr. Catherine Emihovich, dean of the School of Education at the University of Florida and a HERS 2000 graduate, states, "A major benefit of attending the institute is that it provides a broad-based view of executive-level higher education administration. It helps you to think 'beyond the academic' and focus on a multitude of areas that become the core of university leadership roles (e.g., finances, campus and community relationships, student and personnel issues)." The experience she had at HERS pointed to the need for "connecting all the pieces" that one confronts in leadership at the dean level and higher. Having the opportunity to meet and dialogue with motivated women from academic disciplines, as well as human resources and student affairs, the Provost's office, and other areas of the college and university that are important to the success of leadership responsibilities was a good way to prepare for her own campus and its challenges.

For women in Schools and Colleges of Education, there is an annual summer gathering of Women in the Deanship, a subgroup of the American Association of Colleges of Teacher Education (AACTE). This group, which meets each year at the annual AACTE conference, provides women in the deanship, or those aspiring to dean's positions, to share their successes and discuss their challenges in a supportive, non threatening environment. Topics include personnel issues, the dean's role in outreach to the community including the media, institutional advancement and development, and balancing the professional with the personal. Discussions are ongoing throughout the week with hands-on work sessions exploring the complexities of leadership as a woman and many targeted opportunities for professional development and networking.

The American Council on Education (ACE), Office of Women in Higher Education (OWHE) offers the opportunity for women to participate in its National Leadership Forums. These forums play an important role in identifying women for senior-level university positions, particularly college presidencies. Forum topics have included strategic planning, crisis management and resolution, fund-raising and professional development (e.g., resumé review, career mapping, search and selection strategies). These forums are invitational and are held twice a year.

All of these programs and others, such as the Harvard Institutional Management Program, share a focus on preparing women for deanships or other senior administrative posts. It is also noteworthy that these initiatives place a strong emphasis on the importance of mentoring. The chief academic officers who were the participants in the Dean (2004) study were adamant about the critical role that high-quality mentoring plays in accelerating the advancement of women as leaders. Cumulatively, professional development and support programs such as these pursue the critical goal of assuring excellence and equity for women as leaders in higher education.

The Special Education Connection

Analysis of the above literature makes it very clear that there is much overlap between the characteristics, skills and dispositions required for effective leadership by women in higher education and those required by effective special educators. With over fifty years' experience in higher education and special education between us, we have observed that many women who hold deanships or other administrative positions in higher education, particularly in colleges/schools of education, have backgrounds in special education. Subsequently, we began a fact-finding journey with the ultimate goal of helping to create a pool of highly capable women in special education for future leadership positions in Higher Education. We started to gather information about the special education connection in two ways. The first was by planning and implementing a "Women in Leadership" strand at the annual conference of the Teacher Education Division (TED) of the Council for Exceptional Children, which is currently in its third year. This provided an opportunity for doctoral students, women in the various ranks of the professorate, and accomplished women leaders of Schools or Colleges of Education, to come together and discuss leadership from a special education perspective. Sharing administrative, teaching and personal experiences, we began to realize that as special educators we often take on tasks with the strengths associated with our profession (e.g., persistence, collaboration, frustration tolerance), and are recognized by our co-workers as highly capable for doing so. We also possess, as Dan Golman (1998) emphatically points out, the empathy required for effective leadership. Klis and Kossewska (1996) conclude from their study on the structure of personality of special educators that there are higher levels of empathy among special educators than among other groups of teachers.

Empathy is demonstrated in many ways by leaders in higher education. Mainly, it takes the form of thoughtfully considering other peoples' needs and feelings as well as the needs of the organization when decisions are being made. As special educators we have taken particular care to think about how our students and their families feel about their lives, what their needs are and how to move toward positive school outcomes. We are good listeners, demonstrating concern and interest in their lives. We bring this empathy into our work in higher education through behaviors such as legitimizing our colleagues' ideas, facilitating rather than dictating, mentoring a junior faculty member, and sharing our expertise in terms of teaching, research and scholarship.

Paradoxically, the very behaviors that may make women special educators generally effective and sought after as leaders may at times be a cause of concern to them. For example, as special educators, we learn to respect individual differences; often allowing students repeated tries to accomplish a task and accepting alternate ways of problem solving. We sometimes tolerate behaviors that others cannot when it may be better to draw the line and end the conversation. We try to remain flexible at all times, and while this often may be successful, in some cases, we may not make the best decision or allow too much time for decisions to be made. This flexibility may have other consequences, such as being interpreted as not being able to make a decision.

Dialogues on these "special educator" behaviors are healthy for us, and continue to let us reflect and grow as we move toward leadership in our respective colleges, universities, schools, agencies and organizations. Balancing the needs of an organization and the people who staff it is challenging, and the more we learn about the effectiveness of our behaviors, the more successful we will be in accomplishing our vision and goals.

A more in-depth qualitative study to learn more about the special education connection is currently underway. In a set of recent interviews with women either currently or formerly in deanship roles, information has been gathered on perceptions of skills and dispositions associated with being a special educator, and the impact it had on their leadership ascent and effectiveness as well as their personal lives (Lupi, 2004). A preliminary analysis of the interview data reveals that there is a clear set of skills and dispositions that woman leaders possess that is directly connected to their backgrounds and preparation as special educators. These include the ability to persevere, a high level of personal commitment, patience, ability to adapt to change, awareness of the need for consultation and collaboration, frequent recognition and reward for the accomplishments of others, and a strong sense of respect for individual differences. These dispositions and skills are consistent with the literature on effective leadership traits of women and, when brought to the higher education institutional table, can be extremely productive.

Summary

While women leaders have made progress at all levels of university leadership, there are still many roads left to travel (Johnson, 1993). In writing this chapter we discovered many motivators that propel women forward to leadership roles. These generally fit into the "Three P's: Personal, Practical and Professional"."Personal reasons are broad and varied, often determined by culture, ethnicity, religious beliefs and life's experiences and extenuating circumstances. They can include a need for a new challenge, ambition, wanting to help others, or even a need to control. Practical reasons include the financial and family factors discussed earlier. Professional reasons may simply be that leadership is an "excellent opportunity" or come from the urging and support of mentors who regard us as highly capable of doing the job. For others, the call to altruism (e.g..,"This job is important so I'm going to tackle it.") moves them into leadership positions.

As we looked at the Three P's, we once again were drawn to the special education connection. In a recent special education doctoral seminar led by co-uthor Martin, she explored this connection further. Asking the students, male and female, for their descriptors of leadership, their responses included passion, vision, motivation, sincerity, flexibility, honesty, humor, communication, trust and ability to develop good relationships. When asked to describe the characteristics of a leader, the students stated that a leader needed to be confident, reflective, a multi tasker, a risk taker, a decision maker, assertive, a good listener, resilient, outcome oriented and possessing internal strength. Clearly, these special education students on their pathway to leadership had begun to identify "the connection." mentioning key special educator attributes identified earlier in this chapter. Their responses reflected and reinforced characteristics identified by the women deans in the Lupi (2004) study as basic to the profile of a good special educator and essential for effective leadership. Since women comprise the overwhelming majority of special educators, the potential for recruiting and developing women as future higher education leaders seems great. Interestingly, the male special educators from whom data have been gathered exhibit dispositions and skills more similar to female special educators than to the "traditional" male dispositions and skills. Examination of how this came to be should yield valuable insights into the power of nurture over nature in planning preparation programs for all prospective higher education leaders. Future work should be focused on ways in which these special education connections can be built upon to better understand what needs to be done to strengthen the pool of recruits and develop and support them throughout their careers.

In closing, we realize that despite the enormous strides women have made in assuming executive and high-level administrative positions in institutions of higher education, there still exist many gender-based and other challenges. However, we can take much hope from the role models who already exist and from their willingness to work with others who are preparing for leadership roles. Perhaps nothing will be more important in meeting the challenges than developing a resource network of mentors, both female and male, who can share lessons learned as well as ideas for better approaches to improvement. Women, particularly women in special education, represent a largely untapped resource with special talents that can greatly enhance leadership in higher education. The extent to which that resource will be successfully developed is dependent upon all of us. It is a responsibility that we must not shirk.

References

The Allen Group (2004) Feeling Good: Combining Work and Family. *www.theallengroup.com*

Book, E. W. (2000). *Why the Best Man for the Job Is a Woman.* New York: HarperCollins.

Cook, S. G. (2004). Tips on how to turn inspiration into action. *Women in Higher Education. http://www.wihe.com.* (Retrieved November 29, 2004)

Covey, S., A. Merrill & R. Merrill (1994). *First Things First.* New York: Simon & Schuster.

Dean, D. R. (2004). Priming the pump: CAOs move to college president. *Women in Higher Education, 13*(6), 1-2.

Eagley, A. H., W. Wood & A. B. Diekman (2000). Social role theory of sex differences and similarities: A current appraisal. In T. Eckes & H. M. Trauter (Eds.), *The Developmental Social Psychology of Gender* (123–174). Mahwah, NJ: Lawrence Erlbaum.

Eagley, A. H. & M. C. Johannesen-Schmidt (2001). The leadership styles of women and men. *Journal of Social Issues, 57*(4), 781-797.

Golman, D. (1998). What makes a leader? Reprinted from the *Harvard Business Review, 76,*. 92-102.

Hefferlin, J. (1972). Hauling academic trunks. In Charles Walker (Ed.). *Elements Involved in Academic Change* (1-10). Washington, DC: Association of American Colleges. Higher Education Resource Services, *http://www.Wcwonline.org/portal/higher education.html*. (Retrieved June 19, 2004)

Jacqueline M. (2004). *Women in Higher Education*. *http://www.wihe.com*. (Retrieved January 1, 2004)

Johnson, F. (1993). Women's leadership in higher education: Is the agenda feminist? *CUPA Journal*, 9-14.

Klis, M. & J. Kossewska (1996). *Empathy in the Structure of Personality of Special Educators*. ERIC Document Reproduction Service No. ED346082.

Lupi, M. H. (2004). *Effective women leaders in higher education: The special education connection*. Manuscript in preparation.

Munson, G. (2004). Falsely Accused. *The Chronicle of Higher Education*. *http://chronicle.com ?temp/email.php?id=aujyon976d9g32oed5kmkzb49mopvlaj*. (Retrieved May 26, 2004)

Orman, D. B. (2004). The prospects for working in the dean's office. *Women in Higher Education, 13*(6), 5-6.

Oyinlade, A. O., M. Gelhaus & K. Darboe (2003). Essential behavioral qualities for effective leadership in schools for students who are visually impaired: A national study. *Journal of Visual Impairment and Blindness, 97(3)* ,389-402.

Pearce, W. (2001).The hard work of being a soft manager. *Harvard Business Review on Breakthrough Leadership*, Chapter 5, 89-103.

Rosener, J. B. (1990). Ways women lead. *Harvard Business Review, 68*(6), 119-125. EBSCO Research Databases. (Retrieved October 23, 2003)

Tannenbaum, R. & W. Schmidt (1957). How to choose a leadership pattern. *Harvard Educational Review, 27*, 95–101.

Tucker, A. (1984). *Chairing the academic department: Leadership among peers*. New York: Macmillan Publishing Company

Trower, C.A. (2001). Women without tenure: Part 1. *Science/Next Wave* [electronic version] *http://nextwave.sciencemag.org* (Retrieved May 28, 2004)

Women in Higher Education (2002, July) www.wihe.com (Retrieved February 12, 2003.

CHAPTER TWO

Parents as Leaders:
The Journey of Two Mothers

SUSAN DONOVAN AND MARY SENNE

The term "leader" is multidimensional and takes on special meaning when applied to parents of children with special needs. Although these parents are normally not considered or described as leaders, it has been our experience that being a parent of a child with special needs fosters leadership due to the need to advocate for services and educational support for our children. Being a parent of a child with special needs carries with it a certain set of experiences, skills, knowledge and passion that can move parents into leadership roles. We write this chapter with firsthand knowledge, as we are both mothers of children with special needs.

In each of our life journeys, as we became mothers, we took a detour. We each have a child with special needs; one of us is the parent of a teenager, and the other of a young adult. We also have other children who do not have special needs. When our children with special needs were born, we had the same hopes and dreams for them that we had for our other children. When we realized that our children had different needs, we set out to find answers to help us better understand the nature of our child's disability in order. Becoming a leader was never envisioned as a goal for us in our role as parents.

We acknowledge the many contributions husbands and fathers make to the well-being and support of their children, but for the purposes of this chapter, we will talk as mothers of children with special needs. Mothers share a unique set of indescribable feelings, thoughts and needs that thrusts them into a search for answers. The paths mothers take in their search for answers may lead them in many different directions. This can happen by chance, but more likely they occur because the role of "parent" becomes altered when they are presented with a child who has special needs. They may struggle to maintain a sense of "normalcy" within their families and with the outside world; they may become discouraged and exhausted by the seemingly never-ending obstacles and degenerate into embittered, angry people; or they may become strong advocates for their children and along the way become leaders who are recognized by other parents and the professionals with whom they work.

Mothers of children with disabilities often assume the unique role of advocate/servant, giving service not only to their child but also to the many systems in which the child is involved. These roles, and the behaviors learned while playing them, are shaped by the experiences they face in the early years of parenting. Numerous professionals are involved with your child in those years but the touch point, or the advocacy starting line, is the child's first teacher. Schools pose a different and new set of challenges. While mothers may not be clear about the roles they should be playing in their child's educational plan, and if the teacher or the school system does not provide necessary information, they are often left vulnerable and frustrated. This lack of clarity can confuse mothers especially if there are cultural differences and language barriers. This lack of clear information may prevent mothers from demonstrating the necessary leadership skills and behaviors to actively engage in a complex educational system. The process of advocating for one's child is further complicated by a mother's need to develop new relationships each time her child moves forward to another level of learning. Mothers need to understand their role and learn their place in the process in order to become effective child advocates. The challenge before them is to strike a balance between the hope that their child can achieve to his/her maximum potential and the acceptance of the realities and limitations that their child's disability poses.

Mothers of children with disabilities often follow a different path than that traditionally associated with the development of leaders. It is the influence of the child's issues and needs that drives the evolution of leadership. Curry (2000) talks about the development of a "leader persona" which reflects a conscious self-determination. The beginning of the journey with a child with special needs often does not involve conscious, planned, self-determination. Rather it is the process, over time that leads to this persona.

The perception of oneself as a mother of a child with special needs and the acceptance of one's responsibility can occur immediately, gradually or not at all.

For many of us, leadership emerges and we do not even realize it. We are so busy running the race we often forget that it is a marathon, not a sprint. The raising of a child, any child, with or without a disability, can be seen as a parallel journey between parent and child. Does this journey in and of itself create a leader? How and why do some women become leaders and others do not? What skills and experiences shape the formation of a woman leader? We will attempt to answer some of these questions using our own unique experiences, knowledge and insights. We will define our perception of the role of a woman leader in the context of children with special needs and describe the journey of service as we have experienced it. Much of our focus will be in the area of education. We will review the literature regarding parents as partners in the educational arena and how changes in relationships between parents and professionals in schools may enhance the role of women as parent leaders.

Legal Mandates and Parental Involvement

Family involvement in education opens the door to partnerships with professionals and often provides leadership opportunities for mothers. Many studies provide powerful evidence of the relationship between parent involvement and student performance. The extent to which family members are able to become involved in their children's education is an accurate predictor of a student's achievement (Ammon, Chrispeels, Safran, Sandy, Dear and Reyes, 2000; Ammon-Peretti, 1999; Burts and Dever, 2001; Epstein, 2001; Evans-Schilling, 1999; Katz & Bauch, 1999). Increasingly, families are being viewed in various leadership roles: as active partners and educational leaders at home and school; as active decisionmakers on school boards and advisory councils; and as community and legislative advocates who help schools achieve effective educational offerings (Berger, 2003).

The Individuals with Disabilities Education Act (IDEA) and No Child Left Behind Act (NCLB) share common language that strengthens the role of families in education. These laws support the idea of families working together with professionals as true partners in the educational arena. Family participation in education is viewed by policy makers as crucial in order to develop appropriate educational programs for children as well as to achieve full implementation of the law.

The IDEA has significantly increased the role of families in the education of students with disabilities by emphasizing the role of the family in planning and coordination of services (Sileo, Sileo & Prater, 1998; IDEA, 1997). The IDEA Amendments of 1997 require documentation of active family involvement in the educational process. Additionally, the IDEA stresses the many levels needed for family involvement, including families being viewed as in partnership with professionals. Another significant piece of legislation that has strengthened the role of families in education is the NCLB of 2001. NCLB furthers the commitment to family professional partnerships and contains many requirements for school family communication and engagement and leadership roles for parents and family members.

The requirements in these two laws have focused attention on the important role of the family. The IDEA and the NCLB move beyond school family communication and engagement of families in their child's education, to a deeper, more meaningful collaboration in the decisions, policies and practices of the schools. These changes in relationships between families and professionals in schools increase the opportunities for women to become parent leaders on a par with professionals.

The type of leadership demonstrated by women who have children with special needs arises from the need to serve their child. This form of leadership is closely aligned with a model in business known as "Servant Leadership." This term, developed by Robert Greenleaf (1970), describes a leader as one who wants to serve. Greenleaf contends that this type of leadership can have a profound effect on the quality of society. We will now look at how women in leadership roles, as parents of children with special needs, exhibit this type of leadership.

Characteristics of Leadership

The role of any mother, in a culture, is to meet the basic needs of her child. Children with special needs often have multiple, acute needs that require a great deal of attention. How does a mother learn the skills to provide the needed daily support? From where do the knowledge, the energy and the compassion come? What characteristics and traits make it easier for some women to become servant leaders?

As women leaders we need to be committed to a goal. For us, the ultimate goal has always been to improve the quality of life for our children. We discovered that while striving to attain this ultimate goal, many other goals arose. One goal, initially, was trying to find answers about our children's disabilities. A subsequent goal was looking for ways we could improve his/her chance for success. These goals expanded to a desire to educate others (e.g., teachers, principals, therapists, doctors) about our children's disabilities. If they wish to be viewed as leaders, mothers must have the ability to stay focused. Family members, husbands and other children often compete for equal time. In the following section, we will share our stories with examples of how we became servant leaders.

Our Leadership Journeys

Mary: "By the time my son was three, he had been evaluated by multiple specialists and the recommendations were fairly consistent: he would never develop, never have language, be a strain on the family and therefore should be placed in a residential facility for lifelong support. Residential treatment was not an option for my husband and me. There was never a doubt from that point on that my goal was to support our son, help him develop and integrate him into our family. I began by reading everything available about language acquisition. I asked for information from colleagues with whom I worked in psychiatry, as well as friends, family members and sometimes total strangers. The greatest source of information and support came from other parents who had children with special needs. Three years passed, and we finally received a diagnosis of autism. Throughout my son's first few years, my goal was always for him to develop a way to communicate. If he could get his needs met through communication, his frustration decreased and his social and emotional development would improve. If he could communicate, he could function. There were many distractions, many disappointments and much heartache. My son said his first word at age five. He is fifteen now, and communication is still a priority in his life and mine.

Sue: "After struggling within the school system for a number of years as my daughter grew increasingly discouraged, fell further behind, and lost faith in her abilities, I came to realize it wasn't enough for me to understand her disability. The people working with her needed to understand also, but in my search for answers, I realized I now knew more about her disability and effective ways of working with her than they did. I realized that trying to educate them as a parent was not enough and that I needed to become a professional in the field. I had a vague sense that that the more education I obtained the more prepared I would be to advocate for my daughter and share the knowledge I learned. In my search for answers I enrolled in a Master's degree program in Exceptionality and eventually obtained a doctorate in Special Education. During most of the time I was studying, I was raising my three

daughters as a single parent. Not finishing was not an option. I was committed
to the search."

We realized early in our journeys that leaders bring about change by advocating for what they feel is right, through sharing ideas, expertise and stories.
Families of children with special needs have taken the lead in advocating for
services and rights for their children long before special education became a
reality and something protected by law. On a national level, the Parent Training
and Information Centers (PTIC) and Community Parent Resource Centers
(CPRC) funded by the U.S. Department of Education (USDE) Office of Special Education and Rehabilitative Services (OSERS) have been instrumental in
enhancing the high level of families' informed participation in their children's
education and sharing expertise.

Mary: "Integrating my son into the formal education arena was a task for
which I was not ready. By the time he was five years old, my son was receiving
six hours of therapy a day. Upon entering kindergarten, he was segregated
from general education, placed in a trailer in the back of the school building
with fifteen other children with varying disabilities and one teacher. Spring of
that same school year, the teacher resigned, and the class grew to twenty children and my son had lost much ground. I had to do something. With a bank
loan, family support and much energy, I opened a behavioral center for children with disabilities. Initially, the center was small, serving five students. My
son continued to develop and show improvement. Community support came,
other parents came with their children looking for help and eventually the center became a training site for other therapists. Eventually, I partnered with a
community agency already serving adults with disabilities. Today, the center is
thriving. Although my son is entering high school, and has not attended the
center in six years, I still receive letters and calls from families."

Sue: "After earning my doctoral degree, I worked in a state-level early intervention system in Maine, which at the time was an interagency system with
representatives from many state agencies and departments serving children
with disabilities and their families. It appeared, however, that families had limited representation at the state level. Working with some state funding we were
able to increase the participation of families on the state Interagency Coordi-
nating Council by reimbursing them as consultants for their time on the
Council. We also formed a state Parent Advisory Committee with a small grant
from the Department of Education. This Committee developed a handbook
for families in the early intervention system within the state. During my tenure

as the IDEA Part H Coordinator for Maine, I worked with the Office of Special Education Programs to earmark some of our federal dollars to establish a parent-to-parent information system, which helped reach families in remote sections of the state.

This system shared accurate, up-to-date information for families and the regional parent peers served as advocates at Individual Family Service Plans (IFSP) and Individual Educational Plan (IEP) meetings if needed."

We believe that leaders exhibit perseverance and patience. They are willing to stay the course and work one day at a time, staying focused on their goals. We learned perseverance while searching for answers, working with the system and outside of the system. We learned to start over time and time again because we did not know what to do and giving up just isn't an option when it's your child. We were driven and this drive gave us an incredible ability to follow through on tasks—to search for answers, to seek closure. Dealing with professionals who didn't know what to do, or appeared to be uncaring, we learned tact and patience—not because we felt they deserved it but because it was in the best interest of our children.

Mary: "A close friend of mine gave me a copy of an article describing the Individuals with Disabilities Education Act (IDEA, 1997) just after it was reauthorized. My son was nine years old and I knew he needed to be integrated back into the public school setting. This little bit of knowledge about the law gave me the courage to tackle educating my son. The journey through the public education system was filled with barriers including ignorance, lack of understanding and an inability to communicate. Often I was seen as an intrusion. The feelings of hopelessness, despair and fear for my son continued for a very long time. Gradually, I came to realize that it wasn't that the teachers didn't want to work with me to help my son; many of them didn't have the skills or training to do so. Meetings for my son's educational planning were often confrontational, exhaustive and not productive. Usually, eight to ten school personnel would attend and I would come alone. The decisions were made, the individual education plan was already filled out and I was just asked to sign. A great deal of energy and time seemed to be wasted and the outcome for my son didn't seem to change. I knew then that if I was to work within the school system, I had to know the law. I had to educate myself as to what was appropriate, what was reasonable and how could this be accomplished through partnering and not by alienation. I spent a year learning everything I could about family involvement in education. I attended seminars, workshops, used the internet and spoke with school personnel who were willing to share their knowledge. Along the way, I met a leader in higher education. She invited me to work with her on a federal grant involving families and teachers. The experience reinforced for me the notion of partnership. What I had believed all along about teachers and parents was now being researched and I was a part of it. My frustrations gave way to patience. My perseverance gave me the opportunity to find support and affirmation from leaders in the field of education. That same educator who invited me to be involved in her research later encouraged me to complete my studies. She convinced me that I could work within the higher education system, that I could tackle a doctorate degree the same way I tackled other systems and that all I needed was patience and a great deal of support. In a few short months, I will complete my doctorate in exceptional education. My dissertation topic is preparing teachers to partner with families and the support has been unwavering.

Sue: "When my daughter reached age fifteen, she was exhibiting many of the typical behaviors often seen with students who have learning disabilities. Her self-esteem was at an all-time low and she talked about dropping out of school. I enrolled her in an alternative education program at our local high school, but she arrived home after the first day of school telling me she was in regular classes and was told there was no money to pay for her to go to the alternative placement. When I called the principal, he confirmed what she said. He told me that she was the only student who would be going to a particular out-of-town placement and he couldn't justify bus transportation for one student. At this point I knew I needed to put my outrage aside at the fact that we were not informed of this decision and were left out of a discussion of alternatives. I told him that was not acceptable and my goal was to keep my daughter in school. I proposed that if I could find a work placement for her, he would arrange her classes in the afternoon to accommodate a work/study schedule. He agreed, but said the school had been unsuccessful finding acceptable work placements in the area in the past. My daughter wanted to work in a childcare setting. I began with the phone book and called every childcare or preschool in the area. I eventually found a childcare program that recently opened at a nursing home and was willing to have my daughter visit. I called the principal to tell him I thought I had a placement. At that point he told me he didn't think he could give her afternoon classes after all, "because it wouldn't look good to the other students who were in class all day." I requested a meeting with him and told him I would be contacting members of the school board about what occurred. The next day he called to say her classes were set. She began working in the childcare setting the next week. It was an extremely successful placement. The childcare director became a mentor and role model for my daughter who went on to get an Associates' degree (A.A.) at the director's alma mater."

Creativity is a hallmark of leadership. One who leads must be able to look at problems and issues from different perspectives and be open to different solutions. As parents of children with special needs, creativity and flexibility allowed us to reach solutions that may be blocked by what appear to be insurmountable barriers.

Mary: "When my son was diagnosed in 1994, little was being published about autism. Research was underway in various universities and centers across America, yet the disorder still was not widely recognized. When I began investigating autism, I found differing descriptions, confusing terminology, multiple etiologies and dramatically different approaches to treatment. The body of knowledge around autism was scattered in medical journals, university clinic reports and various professional journals and periodicals. In an attempt to find what would work best for my son, I traveled to seven centers around the United States. It struck me that many cities similar in size to the one in which my family and I lived had at least minimal support for families in the way of information, referrals and recommended specialists. Why did my city not have these kinds of resources? After some investigating, it was discovered that a center two and a half hours away provided technical support, training and information for families with children with a diagnosis of autism. This was a model that made sense to me but it was not realistic that families, including my own, should travel such a distance for a service that was so desperately needed closer to home. The solution was quite clear: have a similar resource center in my own city. I called upon my local legislator, spoke with community leaders, asked other parents to write letters of support, partnered with disability advocates in the community and traveled to the state capital to ask for funding. The center has been open for five years and serves over fifteen hundred families."

Sue: "Working in a state system can stifle creativity. Certain funding streams only pay for certain services. Often families and children are declared ineligible for much-needed services because they did not strictly meet what appears to be an arbitrary rule. While working at the state, I advocated for the use of what was know as "wraparound funding." This was flexible dollars to be spent on things not normally obtainable through normal channels. This creative use of funds allowed families of children with special needs to obtain things not covered by agency funds or Medicaid. For instance, the cost of sign language classes was covered for parents of a child who was deaf, and summer camp experiences were paid for children with disabilities when there was no other identified funding source. When families of children with mental retardation and autism expressed frustration that group homes seemed to be the only option for their children, I worked with another agency to look at solutions. We developed in-home Medicaid waivers which allowed families to have in-home supports for their children, keeping families intact."

Good leaders are also good mentors. Not only do they share their knowledge with others, they in turn seek knowledge from more experienced individuals. Also, to be a good mentor, you must be able to let go of the power you possess through the knowledge you have, in order to share it with others. As parents of children with special needs, often our first information about the system in which we found ourselves was from other parents. Once we mastered the intricacies of the system ourselves, we passed that knowledge on to new families entering the system.

Mary: "Not a day goes by that I am not on a phone call or email with a parent. I once was asked why I am so willing to share my experience and knowledge with parents, teachers and other professionals. Do I ever get tired or discouraged? The answer to these questions really begins with my own experience as a new parent of a child with a disability. The support and guidance I received early on regarding my son seemed to come from individuals who were generous with their time, thoughts, prayers and kind words. These individuals were other parents, aunts, neighbors and teachers. Often, when my son was quite young, and I was grieving and struggling to find answers, a mere stranger would share what knowledge they had or thought they had about autism. The searches to find effective treatments, medications, respite or financial support led me into various systems. Within each system I found a multitude of individuals struggling and working as hard as I was to find answers. The knowledge gained in these experiences allowed me to build the courage and fortitude to keep moving forward with one goal: to provide the best possible support to my son while sharing what I know with others."

Sue: "From my early years as a Head Start teacher through working as a preschool teacher, administrator in a state early intervention system and contract manager who provided early intervention services to military dependents overseas, there were many opportunities to learn from others. In turn, I shared what I learned with others. I learned that it was often more effective to share knowledge with those already connected with a part of the system, rather than trying "impart" my knowledge in a formal manner. Lessons learned in one arena could be applied to another. Mentoring took on many forms; sharing information on a particular intervention, methods of working with the state legislature, how to be successful within a military system and developing interagency agreements."

Moving Toward Leadership: Parent as Professional

When did we start seeing ourselves as leaders? In all candor, "mother as leader" was never envisioned as a reality for us but once we became involved with the many systems that serve our children, we had no choice.

What is it that drives us? Is it a sense of compassion mixed with injustice? Is it the desire to change a system by educating others or is it simply to want for this child what we want for all children? Our development as leaders didn't happen overnight, but rather happened through a series of experiences over time. With each setback, obstacle or accomplishment, we learned and we continue to learn. We became recognized within our communities as leaders in education for children with disabilities. Gradually, we recognized and accepted ourselves as leaders. We have received awards, recognitions and letters of commendation over the years; however, they are not the hallmarks of leadership. Our roles as leaders in service to our own children and others like them are cemented through our relationships with many people. At some point what you have learned goes beyond your own child. We began working with other parents to make sure all children have what they need. We worked to change the system to make it equitable and accommodating. Often when parents are dealing with systems (school systems in particular), they experience inequity. They are not viewed as equals in the relationship with professionals, nor are they viewed as leaders. At some point, though, you discover you can add value to the system. It may begin when you advocate for funding with the state legislature or participate in fund-raising activities at the local level. It may encompass establishing services where there were none or having a vision and the determination to see it through.

As a mother of a child with special needs, your journey to leadership is like the Chinese proverb, "A journey of a thousand miles begins with a single step." The ability to concentrate on one goal at a time, or several goals if necessary, taught us to be focused. Trying to find answers to questions that often had no answers honed our research skills and gradually helped us develop a wealth of knowledge. We learned to multitask, an invaluable skill that grew from doing the "extra things" for our child. We learned to think creatively, to find a door when there wasn't one. When you constantly focus on the goal of helping your child, you become very creative at finding solutions. You'll try anything.

We have learned many things from our journey from new parent to mother/leader, and will continue to do so in the years ahead with the new challenges that confront us and our children. We have learned that mother/leaders serve not only their children, but also those that surround them as well as those that come after them. They provide guidance and counsel when necessary, hold themselves as well as others accountable, advocate for those who can't, assist those families who experience language or cultural barriers, and strive to get the best from those we lead. Most of all, as mother/leaders, we must continue to remind the system that we are all vulnerable to disability, and that respect for individual differences and learning styles must remain valued by those who have been given the responsibility for our children. Our journey will never end.

References

Ammon, M. S., J. Chrispeels, D. Safran, M. V. Sandy, J. Dear & M. Reyes (2000). *Preparing educators for partnerships with pamilies. Report of the advisory task force on educator preparation for parent involvement.* Sacramento: California Commission on Teaching Credentialing. ERIC Document Reproduction Services Ed. 437369.

Ammon, P. & D. Peretti (1999). Preparing constructivist teachers for parent involvement: The developmental teacher education program. In M. S. Ammon (Ed.). *Joining hands: Preparing teachers to make meaningful home-school connections* (16–36) Sacramento: California Department of Education.

Berger, E. H. (2003). *Parents as partners in education: Families and schools working together* (6th ed.). Upper Saddle River, NJ: Prentice Hall.

Burts, D. C. & M. T. Dever (2001). Engaging teacher education students in an authentic parent education project. *Journal of Early Childhood Teacher Education, 22,* 59-62.

Curry, B. (2000). *Women in Power: Pathways to Leadership in Education.* Athene Series in Women's Studies. New York: Teachers College Press.

Epstein, J. L. (2001). *School, Family and Community Partnerships: Preparing Educators and Improving Schools.* Boulder, CO: Westview Press.

Evans-Schilling, D. (1999). Preparing educational leaders to work effectively with families: The parent power project. In M. S. Ammon (Ed.). *Joining hands: Preparing teachers to make meaningful home-school connections.* (16-36). Sacramento: California Department of Education.

Greenleaf, R. (1970). *The Servant as Leader.* Indianapolis, IN: The Robert K. Greenleaf Center for Servant-Leadership.

Katz, L. & J. P. Bauch (1999). The Peabody family involvement initiative: Preparing preservice teachers for family/school collaboration. *The School Community Journal, 9,* 49-69.

Individuals with Disabilities Education Act (IDEA) Amendments of 1997 (1997). Public Law 105–17. 105th Congress. No Child Left Behind (NCLB) Act of 2001 (2002). Public Law 107–110. 107th Congress.

Sileo, T., M. Sileo & M.A. Prater (1998). The role of parents in the education of children with disabilities. *Teaching Exceptional Children, 32*(1), 8-13.

CHAPTER THREE

Leading (and Surviving) an Association

NANCY D. SAFER

For individuals committed to a profession, a field, an industry, a specific cause, or contributing to the general good, employment in a not-for-profit association can offer a satisfying but often overlooked career option. This chapter explores the history and nature of associations in the United States, the opportunities they offer for women and a personal perspective on leading an association.

No other country has an association sector as active and fully developed as that of the United States—most people join at least one voluntary association at some time in their lives. Associations are the largest providers of adult education services in the United States, employ thousands of individuals, and contribute over $100 billion to the economy each year (Ernsthal & Jones, 1996). The social contribution of associations is significant. Americans active in associations devote more than 173 million volunteer hours each year to charitable and community service projects.

The American Society of Association Executives reports more than 25,000 national associations and nearly 150,000 state, local and regional associations or chapters. These include trade associations, individual membership organizations or professional societies, or philanthropic organizations. Most are recognized by the Internal Revenue Service as tax-exempt under Section 501(c)(3 or 6) of the Tax Code.

The essential purpose of an association is to empower its members and allow them to exert influence and accomplish things that can't be accomplished by individuals acting alone. Associations, when effective, present a unified voice that is not easily dismissed. And through this voice associations promulgate ideas concerning an industry, profession or cause in a manner that can capture the attention of legislators as well as the general public (Dunlap, 1989).

Associations typically evolve in a similar manner. They generally begin with a small group of people who have an affinity. The founders usually perform the activities necessary to maintain the organization on a voluntary basis, with expenses covered by the contributions of the members. The organization is volunteer driven, and the key to sustaining the group is communication. Often decisions are made by consensus of all of the founding members. However, if successful, the organization grows in such a way that it becomes too burdensome for volunteers to handle communications and coordination of activities, and too difficult for decisions to be made by the entire group. At this point a decision is made to hire a staff member to perform a particular function, often starting with a part-time person, later evolving into full-time work. At the same time the governance structure of the organization evolves, often to that wherein a board of directors, elected by the members for a specific term of office, assumes responsibility for ensuring that available funds and the activities supported by those funds benefit the members and their industry or profession.

As the organization grows, the needs of different types of members increase the range and variety of activities that are desired, which generally raise several issues for the organization. One is financial—the amount of dues that would be required to cover a more diverse set of activities seems prohibitive, and the organization begins to look for non-dues sources of revenue such as conferences, training events, or subscriptions to the organization's journals. A second is management, and often more specialized staff are added to manage the more diverse array of offerings. As the organization grows larger, the board hires a chief staff executive to hire and supervise other paid staff and day-to-day activities. The structure of the organization at this point in its history is that of a volunteer leadership that changes regularly and an ongoing, more permanent staff. This can lead to different leadership patterns, with some associations remaining volunteer driven, with key decisions related to activities, publications and policies made by the volunteer leadership, while others become more staff-driven, and still others a combination, or shared. Each of these patterns has strengths and challenges (Dunlap, 1989). A volunteer-driven association can be slow in making decisions, and thus less responsive to the changing needs of the profession and its members. A staff-driven association can be insulated from the realities of the day-to-day lives of its members, and similarly unresponsive.

Shared leadership can be difficult to achieve. Key for a successful association executive and staff is learning to negotiate and succeed within the pattern of a particular association, or, when necessary, helping the association move to a more effective pattern.

Challenges for Associations

Like many other sectors, the past decade has brought challenges to the association sector. Changing demographics, technological changes, an expanding number of organizations, changes in the lives of members, and the pace of change itself have impacted associations, and dominated discussions among volunteer and paid association leaders.

Changing demographics. It is well documented that the United States is becoming more diverse, and the American workplace is no exception. Immigration, the movement of women into the workforce, and affirmative action have changed the composition of the workplace. Leadership of the associations has not, however, necessarily reflected the growing diversity of the industry or profession. As a result, newer professionals from diverse backgrounds often feel unwelcome, and may not join or participate in the activities of traditional associations, an important concern for those interested in association leadership.

Technological advances

It has been said that the internet changes everything, and that has certainly been true for association leadership. A key responsibility of association leaders is providing their members with up-to-date information as to developments impacting the industry or profession. With the internet has come an explosion of information available from a variety of sources, sometimes on a real-time basis. Associations have been hard-pressed to maintain their information role for their members, struggling to establish websites and online services comparable to those offered by commercial internet services.

Financial

Individual membership associations generally need to be very conscious of the amount of their dues. However, if costs rise at a higher rate than dues, or if there is a demand for more member services, the association leader must be willing to pursue other sources of revenue to avoid significant dues increases. These include revenue sources such as renting the membership list, offering non-professional services such as insurance, credit cards, or travel discounts through affinity programs, or arranging endorsement or co-branding programs with profit-making organizations. Such arrangements can be controversial within the organization, and require the use of sophisticated skills in the areas of negotiation, mediation and public relations.

Competition from new organizations. Each year new associations are established. At the same time, associations are experiencing competition from different types of organizations performing association-like functions. For example, online communities may compete with associations in terms of industry information and networking. Publishing companies and other for-profit corporations may offer training institutes and workshops. Armed with marketing expertise and budgets, these groups can significantly erode association non-dues revenue and present challenges to even the most creative leader.

Changes in lifestyles

Over the past twenty years, but particularly accelerating during the 1990s, Americans have been less engaged in all types of civic, political, religious and social organizations. With more two-worker families, the explosion of technology and mass media, and increased commuting time due to urban/suburban sprawl and traffic snarls, Americans join fewer organizations, and participate less in the organizations they join (Putnam, 2000). Further, family responsibilities and terrorist fears have made people less willing to be away from home, particularly on weekends. As a result, associations have seen membership numbers dropping, a decline in volunteers for committees or leadership roles, and a drop in convention and meeting attendance.

The pace of change

Finally, advances in technology combined with mass media that instantly reach all corners of the globe have resulted in a rate of change in every sector of society that is unprecedented. Successful organizations at a time of rapid change are organizations that are nimble enough to respond quickly to changing circumstances and opportunities. Associations have traditionally not been nimble organizations due to a variety of factors including unwieldy governance structure, limited development capacity and a reliance on volunteers.

A Special Education Association

Within the field of special education, the Council for Exceptional Children (CEC) illustrates nicely the nature and evolution of associations, as well as the challenges facing associations. The Council was founded in August 1922 by twelve women involved in a summer session at Teacher's College in New York City. Their goal was to improve the availability and quality of education provided to students with special needs. These women reached out to others across the United States and Canada, and the group began meeting annually, providing an opportunity for information exchange and coordination of activities on behalf of students with exceptionalities. To enhance its visibility, the organization affiliated with another association, the National Education Association (NEA), in 1924, holding its annual meetings in conjunction with that group. Early on, the organization realized the difficulties of managing an organization using only volunteers. Minutes of the organization lament the absence of the annual meeting one year when nobody remembered to plan it!

To enhance the services it could offer members, the organization merged with the Special Education Department of the NEA in 1941 and acquired the *Journal of Exceptional Children* in 1942. With growing interest in educational services for students with exceptionalities, the membership grew, and with it a demand for more specialized activities and services. In 1951, the first executive staff member was hired, and given the title of Executive Secretary. State and provincial federations were authorized in 1947, and specialty divisions in 1953. In 1958 the organization was renamed the Council for Exceptional Children. By that time it was a very active organization, with awards to recognize significant contributions to the field of special education and the organization. The first full-time Executive Secretary, later renamed Executive Director, was hired in 1961. A government contract to run an information clearinghouse was obtained in 1966, and a new, practice-focused journal, *Teaching Exceptional Children,* started in 1968.

In 1969, CEC withdrew from the NEA, becoming an independent association. Its governance structure, however, continued to mirror that of the NEA as well as many other organizations with a body of delegates, a board of directors (governors) with a representative from every federation and division, and an executive committee with limited powers and responsibilities. During the 1970s and 1980s, CEC provided significant leadership in advocating for state, provincial and federal laws that guaranteed students with disabilities a free, appropriate, public education. The very successful advocacy efforts of CEC to expand educational opportunities for students with exceptionalities resulted in the emergence or strengthening of organizations that quickly became competitors for the information, professional development and advocacy activities that had attracted new members to CEC throughout its history.

Through the decade of the 1990s, greater specialization within the profession of special education also resulted in greater competition between CEC and its specialty divisions in terms of publications, information, professional development and even advocacy activities. Individual divisions hired paid staff that carried out many of the same functions as the Council, but related to a particular constituency group. Because CEC advocated on behalf of all types of students with disabilities as well as gifted students, and on behalf of multiple professional roles (teacher, administrator, diagnostician, early intervention specialist, teacher educator), developing a consensus on policy issues or positions often proved difficult.

The emergence of the internet also impacted CEC in ways similar to other associations. The internet made a variety of new sources for special education information online and available twenty-four hours a day, seven days a week. Information that CEC had historically provided to its members related to federal legislation, or U.S. Department of Education priorities and activities became available from multiple sources, including Congress and the Department of Education, and commercial enterprises. Further, the internet changed expectations so that individuals expected information to be regularly updated, timely, and easy to read, and people also expected to be able to transact business online.

Finally, demographic trends impacted the Council. First of all, there were generational differences in the preferred ways for accessing information. At the same time, as individuals led increasingly busy lives, they participated less directly in local, state, and provincial units. The same group of volunteer members found themselves in the same offices and roles within these units because there was "nobody else" to run for office, plan a state or provincial conference, or organize the local fundraising events.

Thus, by the millennium, the Council for Exceptional Children was facing some significant issues that were very similar to those facing most associations, but still perplexing and challenging. In response, the Council undertook an intensive study of its governance structure as well as its unit and membership structures. In 2000 the Council changed its governance structure to provide for a twenty-one person Board of Directors elected by the membership, holding fiduciary and policy-making powers and responsibilities. As part of the governance restructuring, the organization deliberately considered the relationship between the volunteer leadership and staff, opting for a shared structure. These changes were significant in scope and made to streamline the organization, allowing it to be more flexible and timely in decision making, while at the same time encouraging more vital, relevant units at the state and provincial units.

The Council for Exceptional Children represents an association that has played an influential role in shaping special education, particularly in the United States., while at the same time experiencing the same evolutionary pattern of growth and the same challenges as other associations. What is unique to the Council is the magnitude of the changes in governance it has made in an effort to survive and thrive in the twenty-first century.

Leadership Skills for Association Leaders

Associations can be complex organizations. Though not-for-profit organizations, many associations have revenues the equivalent of those of small businesses or corporations, with staff ranging from five to more than fifty. Similar to businesses, associations are subject to a variety of laws and regulations in terms of how they manage their finances, comply with employer, postal and tax laws and regulations, manage their benefit programs, and other matters not directly associated with the mission of the organization. Also similar to businesses, associations develop services, programs, and products that they must successfully market and deliver if they are to thrive. At the same time, historically, association executives generally have not come to the association with an M.B.A. or even necessarily business experience. In professional associations, it has been a very common pattern for association staff to come from the profession—sometimes with management experience, but often not the extent of experience that allows them to easily understand the complexity of the day-to-day activities of the organization. Recognizing this, there have been efforts to codify the knowledge needed by association executives. The American Society of Association Executives has developed a certification program with an examination resulting in the credential "Certified Association Executive." A growing number of universities have also developed certification programs for non profit executives. Such programs are increasingly popular, both among individuals who have moved into association management from another field as well as with a growing number of individuals that want to make association management their career, with less concern as to the particular organizations with which they affiliate. Whether through formal programs or other means, there is an important knowledge base about associations that successful association executives must master to responsibly guide the organization.

At the same time, the challenges facing associations that were described in an earlier section seem to require an additional set of leadership skills for an association to survive and thrive. The recent experiences and challenges faced by associations across industries and professions led to research to identify the skills needed by successful association leaders in the twenty-first century. Tecker and Fidler (1993) studied 600 associations using a framework developed by the U.S. Department of Labor for achieving a high-performance workplace. They identified five competencies and seven personal characteristics critical for twenty-first century association executives.

The competencies are:

- Interpersonal skills
- Understanding complex relationships
- Acquiring and using information
- Valuing and using technology
- Deployment of resources

These competencies are necessary if the association executive is to manage an organic organization seeking to meet the needs of members not based on the past, but the ever-changing landscape of the future.

The personal characteristics common to all of the competency areas are:

- Cooperatively builds, effectively articulates and is focused on the vision of what success will look like
- Cultivates and trusts instinct and intuition
- Is opportunistic—asks what is emerging that might be turned to advantage
- Has a holistic, multidimensional perception of the interdependence of people, actions and resources
- Inspires and serves others by providing the tools they need, creating a supportive environment for creative expressions and risk-taking
- Trusts self and others, is open and vulnerable, and speaks with integrity

Clearly the competencies and personal characteristics envisioned for the twenty-first century leaders are different than those of traditional organizations operating vertically and compartmentally with information shared on a "need-to-know" basis and management by control. They assume that future success will be based on interdependence, cooperation, customization and involvement, and focus on the expressed needs of those served.

Women in Association Leadership

Interestingly, many of the competencies and characteristics identified as important for successful association executives in the twenty-first century are similar to those identified in a growing literature that has found that female managers often outshine their male counterparts in terms of overall effectiveness. A recent article in *Business Week Online* stated, "Twenty-five years after women first started pouring into the labor force—and trying to be more like men in every way, from wearing power suits to picking up golf clubs—new research is showing that men ought to be the ones doing more of the imitating. In fact, after years of analyzing what makes leaders most effective and figuring out who's got the Right Stuff, management gurus now know how to boost the odds of getting a great executive: Hire a female" (Sharpe, 2000). In analyzing a number of comprehensive management studies conducted for companies across the country ranging from high-tech to manufacturing to consumer services, the report indicated that "the studies show that women executives, when rated by their peers, underlings and bosses, score higher than their male counterparts on a wide variety of measures—from producing high-quality work to goal-setting to mentoring employees" (Sharpe, 2000). Female managers are perceived as more collaborative and less turf conscious, thus functioning better in environments where teamwork and partnering are important.

Given the intersect between the competencies and characteristics of successful association executives and the skills demonstrated by many female managers, we might expect to find females dominating the association sector. However, despite increases in the past decade, only about a third of the nation's association executives are female. Furthermore, most female CEO's are in smaller associations, where they may be the only staff member, or supervise only a handful of staff. They are also much more likely to be found in professional associations than in trade associations.

Female association executives historically have earned significantly less than their male counterparts. In part this is related to the fact that they are more likely to be found in smaller associations offering less in terms of executive compensation. However, when comparisons are made between men and women within association size categories, women still lag behind—more so in larger associations, particularly in trade associations (Sharpe, 2000).

Thus, as we define successful twenty-first century association executives, there is evidence to suggest that many women can bring to leadership roles the personal characteristics and skills most important to successful associations. Unless there are significant changes, however, it is unlikely that the full leadership potential of women for associations will be realized. What kinds of changes are necessary? Certainly the pool of candidates is one area to examine. And in association management there certainly is the possibility of a pipeline issue—that is to say, that while more females have entered association management in past decades, they are still working their way through the ranks of particular associations, or from smaller to larger associations in terms of responsibilities. However, as noted earlier, associations have historically hired executives from within the profession. Thus, in many instances it may be possible to broaden the pool of female candidates by looking beyond the association community to female managers within the profession, including government, higher education, or other administrators in relevant agencies and fields.

The search process itself also needs to be examined. The board of directors, often assisted by a search firm or consultant, generally selects chief association executives. Association search firms tend to be comprised of or run by former association executives, and thus, given the gender characteristics of the field, are primarily male. Further their contact pool within the association world may also be predominantly male. Thus, while good search consultants scrupulously consider the credentials of the full range of candidates in order to identify a diverse "short list," there may be an unrecognized bias in terms of outreach that impacts the pool of applicants. In addition, initial interviews are generally conducted by the search consultant, who may, without realizing it, warm to candidates who are "like me" in terms of style and experiences and move them forward in the process.

Finally there is the board interview and selection process, where, as in business, lots of subtle factors can come into play. According to the co director of Simmons University's Center on Gender & Organization, organizations may say they want collaborative leaders, but they still hold deep-seated beliefs that top managers need to be heroic figures (Sharpe, 2000). Thus, a more assertive male candidate may present himself as the decisive panacea for any perceived problems of the association, by describing what "he" has done and would do. On the other hand, a female candidate with a more collaborative style may hesitate to take credit for past accomplishments, even if she led the group that achieved

them, and may speak of how she will facilitate and work with the staff to address association issues. It may be hard for the board to resist the hero unless
they have carefully considered not just what they hope the next executive will
accomplish, but also the range of skills, including interpersonal skills, that the
individual must demonstrate. This may mean more involvement by the board
up front as well as more guidance to the search firm as to the types of questions
that should be asked of the candidates as well as candidates' references. The
board must clarify for the search consultant what leadership skills and qualities
they are looking for, the range of sources they think should be tapped in recruiting candidates, and what they want to know about prospective candidates. Finally, the board should try to keep a focus on the competencies that will be
needed to accomplish the goals they have set within the dynamics of their association, working with their members and staff.

Associations are very much "people-focused organizations." Thus, in many
instances female candidates with strong collaborative and interpersonal skills
should be top contenders for top-level association positions.

Personal Perspective—Special Educators in the World of Associations

Like many other association executives I know, I never imagined early in my
career that I would someday lead a major special education professional association. Though I knew that professional and non-profit organizations were important, I never thought much about staff positions in such organizations. The
people I associated with such organizations were the volunteers—the president
who sent me a message in a newsletter, the person who called to ask for a dona-
tion, or, as a resident of the Washington, DC area, the staff employed to handle
advocacy and governmental relations. I wasn't aware of the many staff roles
that supported the volunteers nor had I thought about the skills needed by association staff. That changed when, having spent seventeen years at the U.S.
Department of Education in various management positions, my feeling it was
time for a career change coincided with an ad for a newly created position at the
Council for Exceptional Children, an organization I had belonged to my entire
professional career. I applied and was hired as the Deputy Executive Director,
viewing it as an opportunity to learn more about associations. Three months
after I began that position, circumstances resulted in my becoming first the In-
terim, then the Executive Director of CEC. It was on-the-job training in every
sense of the word, and an opportunity to learn firsthand what skills were neces-

sary to lead an association, and how those matched the skills of a special education professional.

Over the years I learned that there is much overlap in the characteristics and skills that make a good special educator and those needed by a good association staff member. Both groups share a commitment to a mission, in the case of CEC, to the mission of improving the lives of students with exceptionalities, their families and those who serve them. During my time at CEC I was struck by the dedication of staff, whether or not they were special educators, to the mission of the organization. They were attracted to the organization and stayed because they wanted to make a difference.

Good special educators are collaborative, understand the importance of teams and have the skills to work well with other educators and professionals, as well as with parents. Similarly, association staff must be able to work collaboratively with other staff as well as volunteer leaders. Many associations are relatively small in terms of staff size, and most have at least one "big event" each year—the annual convention. Staff members wear many hats, and must pull together to get things done, whether or not a task is a part of his or her job description. The person who prefers to work alone and to do only his or her job generally doesn't work well in an association.

Special educators expect the unexpected, and are good at crisis management. A variety of events can impact an association, and staff must be able to respond quickly to new requests and circumstances. During my tenure at CEC we dealt with a continually leaking building, a blizzard that stranded staff right before a governance meeting, changes in special education laws that significantly impacted the lives of our members, a host of legal issues, media attacks on the cost of special education and its effectiveness, the aftermath of the terrorist attacks that significantly disrupted mailing operations as well as an annual convention planned for New York City and a variety of other unanticipated events. These, combined with planned changes such as a major restructuring of the organization's governance and unit structure, rapid changes in the use of technology and the relocation of the headquarters operations, resulted in an environment that was constantly changing, requiring a high level of adaptability and skill at coping with uncertainty.

The ability to take satisfaction in the accomplishments of others is a characteristic of special educators and association staff. A teacher may work for days teaching a child a skill, but mastery belongs to the child, and the teacher is quick to praise the child for "his" or "her" accomplishment. Similarly, it is the job of association staff to facilitate the success of the member leaders, and to recognize their success. Though many volunteer leaders acknowledge and thank association staff for their contributions to the organization, the organization exists for the benefit of its members, and its accomplishments are their accomplishments. Thus, the association environment is not a good match for those who need individual recognition for all of their work.

Special educators are used to working with attorneys. In an increasingly litigious and regulated world, associations can easily find themselves brushing up against labor laws, civil rights laws, interstate commerce laws, antitrust laws and tax laws governing not-for-profit organizations. A regular feature of *Association Management,* the journal of the American Society of Association Executives, is a legal column outlining potential legal perils for associations. Thus prudent association executives, like special education administrators, regularly consult with their attorneys as they consider particular activities or actions, and have their attorneys on "speed dial" for unexpected legal crises.

There are also aspects of association management that are not a natural match with the training of special educators. As noted above, associations are in many ways like small businesses, and the day-to-day activities of association executives are very business oriented. They focus on direct mail marketing, membership growth, publication sales, how many people will come to the annual convention, non-dues revenue and, most of all, on the bottom line. Some organizations do have a hefty reserve fund, though this has never been true for CEC. Thus, unanticipated circumstance raised both management and financial concerns, and a great deal of anxiety—would a bad convention, a lawsuit, or a drop in membership necessitate a reduction in staff, services or worse? Many days I thought that the organization and I would both have been better served if I had a degree in business rather than special education. And many days I felt very removed from the world of students with exceptionalities and those who served them, our members. That disconnect is probably greatest for association executives that come from the profession or industry, less so for those choosing association management as a lifelong career path.

Finally, there are features of associations that require adjustments for staff regardless of their training and experience. One of these has to do with the constant change in volunteer leadership. Changes in leadership naturally bring some level of anxiety to the staff of an organization. While in the Federal government I saw the stress that took hold among the civil service ranks every four years, even when there was no change of party. In associations, the presidency changes every one to two years. I was privileged to work with some wonderful presidents during my time at CEC, yet each came with a different personality, different goals and a different leadership style, requiring at least some adjustment. In educational terms, it is like a school having a new principal every year. Regardless of the strengths of the principals, there are still adjustments required. Another feature, also related to the role member leaders play in the organization, relates to the schedule of weekend events. Many association activities are scheduled on weekends to accommodate the work schedules of member volunteers. This includes board meetings, committee meetings, state or provincial unit meetings, fund-raising events, professional development activities and portions of the annual convention. Though no particular meeting is the issue, cumulatively for association staff, this can impact family life, and pose real problems for single parents with young children.

At some time during any given year, most association staff are involved in some way in weekend events. Association executives, however, are most impacted, with some spending one to two weekends a month involved in association activities. It is definitely a consideration for individuals considering association staff positions, and may particularly be a factor for women with family responsibilities.

Conclusion

Despite the many associations and nonprofit organizations in this country, work in the association/nonprofit sector is often considered more in voluntary terms than as a career choice. Nonetheless, it can be a satisfying job experience providing an opportunity to both influence and serve a particular cause or profession. The past twenty-five years have seen the development of the profession of association management and the identification of knowledge and skills important for association executives. The changes and challenges of the past decade have further refined those skills in a way that matches the preferred management style of many women. Though association executives are still disproportionately male, this may change, particularly if women who have achieved leadership positions in other sectors such as higher education or government agencies are attracted to association management.

Traditionally many of us have thought of career paths in very linear terms—one selects a career and a type of organization, pursues success and fulfillment within that arena, and then retires. There is, however, another model that is more constructivist in nature, allowing the possibility of applying a set of skills developed in one role to another, then growing and acquiring new skills in that new role, in a lifelong cycle of change and growth. In *Composing a Life* (1989), Mary Catherine Bateson elucidates this perspective. In this book she explores the improvisations that often take women from one role to another in their careers, creating a richness of experiences and growth despite the discontinuities an outsider might see applying a traditional lens. Applying these two perspectives, association work can be a career or a step in a career. In either case it can offer challenge and growth, an opportunity to serve a profession or a cause, and be a source of close and lasting relationships.

References

American Society of Association Executives (2003). *ASAE Compensation Survey.* Washington, DC: American Society of Association Executives.

American Society of Association Executives Website. (2003). *Association Quick Facts.* http://*www.asaenet.org* (Accessed March 10, 2004).

Bateson, M. C. (1989). *Composing a Life.* New York: Grove Press.

Dunlap, J. J. (1989). *Leading the Association.* Washington, DC: Foundation of the American Society of Association Executives.

Ernstthal, H. L. & B. Jones (1996). *Principles of Association Management.* Washington, DC: American Society of Association Executives.

Putnam, R. (2000). *Bowling Alone.* New York: Simon & Schuster.

Sharpe, R. (2000). As leaders, women rule. *Business Week Online,*Boston. *http://www.businessweek* (Accessed April 6, 2004).

Tecker, G. & M. Fidler (1993). *Successful Association Leadership: Dimensions of 21st Century Competency for the CEO.* Washington, DC: American Society of Association Executives.

CHAPTER FOUR

Three CEC Presidents Speak on Leadership

DIANE JOHNSON, PAMELA GILLET AND LINDA MARSAL

Leadership and the Organization

Serving as the elected president of a professional organization provides the opportunity to apply skills that are part of your profession, gain additional skills that will transfer to the workplace and other life settings, meet many individuals with the same commitment and values and allow for impact on public policy and advocacy. The three authors of this chapter each served as president of the Council for Exceptional Children (CEC), the largest international professional organization dedicated to improving educational outcomes for individuals with exceptionalities, students with disabilities and/or gifted students. Each arrived at this office through different life and professional experiences.

Mendez-Morse (1993) stated that there is a connection between leaders' values or beliefs and their vision for their organizations. In a review of leadership literature to identify characteristics that appear to facilitate or impede the implementation of school improvement interventions, especially those likely to benefit at-risk students, six characteristics of leaders of educational change were identified. These six characteristics are having vision, believing that the schools are for learning, valuing human resources, being a skilled communicator and listener, acting proactively and taking risks.

Each of the chapter authors began a career in education with the desire to make a difference for children. Each had opportunities to provide leadership as a classroom teacher, and later through a variety of administrative positions within public education and related education settings. These six characteristics, along with the concept of meeting the needs of at-risk students, were part of the make up of each of the authors in their professional roles. They worked in public education during a time of tremendous change, focusing on access and transitioning into the school reform and accountability movements.

Organizational Leadership

Specific characteristics for organizational leaders were described in the following passage from the Mid-America Association of Educational Opportunity Program Personnel l (MAEOPP) Emerging Leaders Institute Resource Manual for Non-Profit Organizations.

> Leadership means many things to many leaders. Many sources converge on a handful of characteristics; several sources further agree that non-profit board leadership is a special brand of leadership. Board leaders in general must be fair and tough, show sensitivity, maintain enthusiasm, provide consistent direction, act reliably and exhibit controlled ambition.
>
> Leaders must also provide an inclusive and encouraging environment so that board members feel comfortable working among the group—board members should not be intimidated into inactivity out of fear or embarrassment. Leaders should: be committed to serving the cause; be team-players; work well with others and generally like people; think objectively and put others' needs ahead of their own; be flexible about change, yet realistic and practical when considering feasibility issues; exhibit patience, maturity and tolerance; and work diligently. (MAEOPP Emerging Leaders Institute Resource Manual for Non-Profit Organizations, 2004, Chapter 2)

The authors found in the role as president that these skills and characteristics for board leadership also applied. CEC as an organization had the same forces exerted from the community for access and accountability as the education system, creating common elements between professional and organizational leadership for these presidents. The link between their profession and the dedication to common ideals within the professional organization allowed the authors to work within both structures simultaneously.

Applying professional skills to organizational leadership

The evaluation of transfer of learning from the classroom to a naturalized setting where academic skills are used to accomplish tasks encountered in everyday situations has been a proven technique to assess the acquisition of certain academic skills by children and youth, especially those with severe disabilities. The application of the principle to transfer of skills learned pertains to adult learning as well. Leadership skills developed and refined in special education administrative positions are readily applied to sets of circumstances faced by leaders of an international special education organization. As past presidents of CEC, we found that the skills necessary to make informed administrative decisions and to provide program direction in school district matters were quite usable in reading a professional member-based organization structure. The skill to openly listen to all opinions and concerns presented on topics relative to budget, program, class size and teaching conditions as special education administrators proved to be easily transferable in the decision-making process during our presidential terms.

Two-way communication is an essential characteristic of an educational leader. Taking time to request "input" from diverse groups, weighing all comments, and then acting in an informed, responsible manner was the process applied during our terms as president when selecting appropriate activities for the organization's seventy-fifth anniversary celebration, addressing a major professional staffing situation, and organizing a significant study focusing on the current status of special education teaching conditions. As each of us worked to address the major issues described above, we were reminded how important it is to ensure that the decision is communicated to all stakeholders in a timely and efficient manner. The focus of special education has always been on the individual student. However, as a special education administrator and leader of a special education organization, the focus shifts to the good of the district and the organization. All decisions made had the larger focus knowing full well that there would be individuals and factions who would not agree. As a leader in both settings, the integrity of the whole outweighed the parts. While the decision made may not have been the one chosen by all, by using the two-way communication process described, the rationale and knowledge of the decision was available to all and the decision made was more easily understood.

The driving force that permitted the determination and selection of goals during our presidencies and throughout our special education administrative roles was the provision of more appropriate services for exceptional children and youth. With this focus, we were able to select issues for study, develop strategies to solve issues, and support funding increases. That would lead to better service for students with disabilities.

When proposals were made in the professional organization concerning budget line items, program direction, professional development activities and publications, the first question we raised in the role of president was, "How does this impact the lives of children with special needs?" The plan of action was dependent on the answer to this question regardless of who made the recommendation.

The knowledge base of special education we had as administrators and the experience with the practical application of the knowledge and skills was critical in our functioning in a one-year presidential term. We had to "hit the ground running" as we prepared the annual agenda for the organization. Just as annual goals are a mandated portion of the student's individual education plan (IEP), so are they essential as an administrator and organizational president. There were program and organizational goals, as well as those set for us individually. Goal setting affords a focused approach to decision making, especially when working with so many constituent groups found in the school system and professional organization. Goals also enable priorities to be determined when many divergent requests are being made of the educational leader. Goals form the framework by which the administrator and president can clearly articulate to all involved the forward movement of the district or organization. Allocation of funds for requests are much more objectively handled when it must be demonstrated that the activity/position funded will contribute to goal actualization.

The use of goals should be a "natural" for all special educators, especially those in leadership positions. The student's IEP changes to a program plan and budget for the school administrator and then becomes incorporated as the strategic plan for the professional organization. Actually, goal setting proved to be even more important with the professional organization than in the school system, since the term of president was limited and predetermined. Due to this limitation of time in the presidential sequence (three years), it was imperative that precise, measurable goals be set with individual and organization-based activities that could be specifically evaluated on a set time schedule. Establishing goals in both positions supported self-direction in the leadership roles. The goals, their related activities, and status of attainment provided the road map so that all involved could easily follow the action plan.

Skills used by the special education administrator in chairing IEP conferences have direct applicability to the role responsibilities needed as president of a professional organization. As chair of the IEP conference, the administrator works with varying constituents, all representing the student, but often seeing the student's diagnostic profile, learning style and needs in a different way. The administrator must provide equal access to information to foster open communication, summarize salient points, apply regulatory processes and ultimately achieve consensus.

Modeling the IEP process, the president of an organization uses small groups to study issues, develop premises and prepare recommendations for the betterment of the organization. Experience with overseeing the IEP process provides the organization leader with a procedure applicable to consensus - building among the divergent opinions and groups within the professional organization. This building of consensus and development of a commitment to a common cause is definitely important in a membership-based organization concerned with advocacy, a national special education agenda, education publications and multicultural issues.

At the conclusion of a successful IEP conference, certain participants become responsible for implementing the various decisions made by the group. The organization leader also has the role of ensuring that the delegation of authority is transferred to members so that ownership is vested to all to carry out the campaigns of the professional organization. If the members are not involved and if the organization is not providing options in service to meet the membership's needs, the organization loses its advantage as an influencing agent.

Since today's special education administrator has a varied cadre of responsibilities, the skill of organization is paramount. Setting priorities, knowing when to use special education regulations to the fullest and when to meet the "intent," allotting timelines for grant preparation, and delivering the most effective professional development options all need to be accomplished, often with a firmly set timeframe dictated by a regulation, policy or notification date. The decision-making process, as well as the informing of all constituents about developments, must be well organized and require succinct and clear communication in both verbal and written form.

In many administrative situations in school systems, the administrator is requested to put forth proposals to various bodies: the district council, advisory groups, and boards of education, to name a few. The format is written and involves a background statement, area of study, problem needs, technical information, alternatives, the proposal implications (policy, financial, personnel) and the recommended action. This same type of format can be applied within the professional organization when major agenda items are being considered.

An effective educational leader is constantly analyzing cause and effect relationships. As leaders in school systems, we prepare the most appropriate educational plan based on a student's diagnostic profile and responses to various situational encounters. The student's learning characteristics and behavior styles determine the pedagogy. We then monitor changes in the behavior resulting from the applied teaching styles, techniques and materials adaptation.

After participating in a series of professional development activities, the administrator also analyzes the impact of the training on actual teaching. Observing how changes in teaching approaches positively affect student's growth patterns assists in refining and changing future staff training programs. In the professional organization, the leaders watch for the same type of systemic relationships, member response to an advocacy position proposed, enrollment in professional development activities, sale of publications and attendance at organization-sponsored conventions and conferences. Being able to see the relationship of products to actions assists the president of an organization in keeping the organization fluid and making the necessary changes based on the member's responses. The president is challenged to consistently access members' needs in providing varied services and products.

Advocacy skills are required in both administrative and organizational leadership positions. Advocacy efforts provide a road map that guides program initiative and implementation through minefields that are certain to evolve, and helps program developers maintain focus.

Advocacy leaders are change agents. The goal of advocacy for both schools and professional organizations includes protection of appropriate educational programs and services; quality of education instruction; adequacy of specially trained personnel; stability of home, school and community relationships; and the enhancement of the student's self-concept. Professional organizations have more scope and therefore can design regional and/or national advocacy campaigns. They legitimize local-based efforts and provide a broad base for support. However, there is no substitute for a small school-based or district team of hardy advocates willing to invest the time and energy necessary to make changes or protect current systems. To lead in the advocacy movement, the administrator/organizational leader may often be the singular spokesperson willing to search for the opportunities and take the risks to lead the way for others to follow.

The lasting work of a dynamic leader is the imprint we leave on others; it is the desire to become a future leader. Sharing knowledge of special education tenets and legal implications as well as processes applied to administrative tasks and responsibilities with aspiring administrators is a true indicator of a successful confident administrator. Ensuring others will be there to lead should be paramount in the administrator's leadership career. The same need for mentorship exists with the professional organization, perhaps even more so as these positions are volunteer and not salaried. There are many capable members in organizations at all levels who need to be recognized and instructed, mentored and fully supported as they assume that initial leadership position.

Mentoring is more important today in professional organizations than in the past. Today, many of those we may look to as future leaders just do not see the importance of a professional organization leadership role. Someone else is there to do it. The leader of a school system needs to ensure that professionals practicing in their classrooms, schools and district-wide programs see the need to use their skills at another level—the professional organization. Personal time spent with selected individuals sharing expertise, information bases, and "how-to" is the proven way for a leader in either type of position to ensure others will follow. Illustrating how the individual's current skills and knowledge can be applied to this new area helps them realize it is truly application, not an entirely new set of knowledge and skills, that must be mastered.

Experience as a special education administrator was essential to the successful terms in the office of president of our professional organization. The manner in which problems are identified, alternatives explored, programs developed, consensus reached, and services rendered calls for the same type of leadership skills necessary to function in the role of a special education administrator. The settings may be different, the organizational protocols unique, the substance of the issues distinctive and the constituents diverse, yet the same types of leadership styles and skill are applicable to both school-based and organizational positions.

Successful leaders in school-based and organizational positions work with others to advance the position of their schools and organizations as advocates for the appropriate education of children and youth with exceptionalities, to deliver quality professional services to our staff and members, to influence public policy, and to ensure representation of children and youth from diverse ethnic and multicultural backgrounds. All resulting in improved services for all children and youth.

Service commitment an essential ingredient

The culture of an organization can provide a link to strong leadership and accomplishment of objectives. A strong sense of service was important and part of the orientation for these presidents. Participation in leadership of CEC is a volunteer activity, requiring balancing of personal life and family considerations with job responsibilities to be able to serve. Someone at a leadership conference once said that their favorite and most contributed to charity was CEC because of the personal time and financial resources that they invested. The individual leader's view of service is an important consideration, especially in a volunteer organization such as CEC. If the mission is not clear and compatible with the values of the individual, then the participation in the organization will not be satisfying, nor will this individual become an effective leader within the organization.

A sense of community, the shared interest in the common good, was also a part of the overall culture within CEC and shared by these presidents. The participation within the leadership structure by many who are well known through publications and research, collaboratively with teachers, administrators and other field-based practitioners, added resources and strength for decision making to improve the organization.

Strength of the organization is the commitment to improving professional practice and conditions of teaching. While improved outcomes for students are a paramount consideration, the professionals who work with them are also well served by the organization, and part of the focus for these presidents. Development of the standards for professional practice was a shared responsibility with public school, higher education, and researchers working together. These standards of practice, with input from across the organization, have been adopted my many licensing agencies. These standards have led to teacher recognition and common elements of personnel preparation and professional development in university and school districts in many locations. These standards also helped determine the professional development provided by the organization.

Shared community and service orientation is part of the culture of CEC, allowing leaders and members to know that when they meet fellow CEC members far from their local area, they will have a common understanding of mission and purpose, a common place to start a conversation, and a common interest in sharing resources and strategies. This community and service orientation is a building block for leadership and continued growth of the organization.

As president, this community of members was available as a resource in meeting the goals of the organization.

On Leadership and Becoming President

A brief review of the individual journeys of each of the authors shows the common elements that led them to CEC and to their roles as president. Linda Marsal's personal career reflection captures the leadership characteristics, the relationship to national events and the role CEC played in personal, professional and leadership development.

Pam Gillet

Being a first-year general classroom teacher, I was faced with the challenge of a class of unique children having a wide variance in age and disabilities. These challenges sent me returning to school to pursue additional training, and through professors and another student I learned of the Council for Exceptional Children and the training networking this organization could provide.

As I gained more experience in the classroom and pursued graduate-level coursework, I began to realize instead of just trying to "change" children, systems had to change. For this reason, I entered special education administration, as challenges are always present and with the quest to design programs and make refinements in those currently offered, college coursework proved not to be enough. The professional organization provided me with additional training opportunities, a national perspective and the vehicle to expand professional networking. My professional organization benefited me so greatly, I wanted to offer my services in return, and so the pathway to organizational leadership positions began.

Diane Johnson

Growing up in a household where service and giving back to the community were important, and practiced, I was always aware of the need for active participation as part of your involvement in the community, whether in school, job or extracurricular activities. My mother was a teacher who began working with special needs students long before there was federal legislation (PL 94–142). Part of her professional involvement was with CEC, which for me was something that she did as part of her career. After graduating from college, my first job was teaching home economics in a middle school in Maryland. I had an extra planning period one day per week and was asked to provide instruction to the girls from the "special education department" during that time. Because I had spent time with my mother's students during school activities, I agreed. The special education teacher usually came with the students, and the activities were very hands-on, so this experience was a positive one.

A year later, after moving back to Florida, when I reported to the school, I found that I had been moved to a new position as a teacher of a special education class, rather than the class that I thought I would be teaching. I accepted the position, but found that teaching all subjects to a group of middle school students with a variety of disabilities was much more challenging than my limited experience in Maryland. Some summer training was provided through the Department of Education, and I also took some university classes. A CEC chapter was formed that year, and that and the classes got me through the year. This change in teaching assignment led to a decision to return to the university for a graduate degree in special education, and continued my involvement with CEC. As I moved into an administrative position working with teachers in professional development, I found that the CEC connection was even more important in terms of information and resources. My boss was on the state CEC board, and decided that I would be a good newsletter editor. With this entrance onto the state board began my journey in CEC leadership, which led to a variety of state offices and eventually to CEC president.

Linda Marsal

How did I become a leader in special education? I'm not really sure. I started out wanting to be a teacher—wanting my students to learn to read—wanting to do a good job—wanting to be successful in my chosen career. I never planned on being a leader. It just happened. For me it happened because of strong mentoring relationships. It happened because others took the time to share their knowledge and skills. It happened because someone took the time to push, encourage and pave the way. It happened because someone saw that I had possibilities. My story is their story.

After graduating I found a job as a teacher of junior-high-age students with mental retardation in a rural school system. My classroom was located away from the main school building. Each day, I marched my students to the playground, lunchroom, and out to meet the busses in the afternoon. I rarely spoke to the other teachers in the school. As a high-school-trained teacher in English and social studies, I was afraid they would find out just how little I knew about teaching children with mental retardation at the junior high level. I certainly didn't know how to teach reading. I had thought when I took the job that most children could read in junior high. Most children could however, the ones I taught could not. That lack of knowledge created a struggle for me during my first year of teaching. I promised myself if I ever got through that first year I'd learn how to teach reading by the second!

In the rural education district where I worked I felt so alone. In the group of CEC members in Charlotte I found other teachers who were doing the same things I was doing. I was no longer alone.

I found, within my varied roles in the association, people who have good hearts and who have shared values with me. We have worked together to bring about changes that benefit children and the adults who serve them. I found people who valued my contributions to the association and me. I built lasting relationships with many of them. I found many mentors along the way.

Pam Gillet reached out and encouraged me to consider the presidency of CEC. Pam was the president of CEC at that time. I could not visualize myself in Pam's role. Pam did. Diane Johnson always made the time to listen to the questions of an inexperienced board member who was learning the ropes. Executive Director Nancy Safer asked me just what I really wanted to accomplish the year I was CEC president. I was interested in improving things for teachers in the classroom. Nancy worked with her staff and me to see that CEC did a study on the teaching conditions in special education.

So many people have mentored me and made a significant difference in my life. All are individuals with strong personal, emotional and professional ties who are leaders in the field of education. Each of these people has a strong knowledge base of our craft—education. Their leadership is coupled with a passion for excellence, and a strong work ethic. To that mix add family values, cognitive and creative energy, self-confidence, organizational skills, the ability to see opportunities where others see problems, and dissatisfaction with the status quo. With my mentors I have formed lifelong professional and personal relationships. They have made a difference in my life.

Conclusion

There are many parallels between the leadership roles served in their profession and their role as president of CEC. The characteristics and skills of both are often interchangeable. The path to leadership was different for each president, but the shared commitment to the purposes of the organization and a willingness to serve were the same.

It is important to share knowledge, experiences and encouragement with others so that leaders will continue to be willing to serve. A professional organization provides an avenue for growth and continued adventures, and leadership is an important part of moving every community forward.

The small word "yes" is the greatest positive contributor to leadership opportunities. If you are willing to accept responsibility for one task within an organization when asked, this will allow you to begin a leadership journey of your own. Say yes to an opportunity today, and be ready to share your story and experiences tomorrow.

References

Council for Exceptional Children (2004). *http://www.cec.sped.org* (Accessed June 2, 2004)

Mendez-Morse, S. (1993). "Leadership Characteristics that Facilitate School Change." Southwest Educational Development Laboratory. *http://www.sedl.org/change/leadership* (Accessed May 22, 2004)

Mid-America Association of Educational Opportunity Program Personnel (MAEOPP) Emerging Leaders Institute (ELI) Resource Manual for Non-Profit Organizations. *http://www.geocities.com/eli_maeopp/Resource_manual* (Accessed May 15, 2004)

CHAPTER FIVE

Leading in an Age of Change: A Dean's Reflection

DEBORAH A. SHANLEY

This year marks eleven years of serving in a dean's position, on two different campuses, and I jumped at the idea of stepping back to reflect on past events and experiences that shaped my style of leadership. The task of contributing these ideas in writing provided the opportunity to critically reflect on how I approached developing a shared vision and mission with a faculty on one campus. Did I have a sense of what, in my background and professional development in the field of special education, may have influenced the paths I traveled and impacted my decisions along the way?

There were many different philosophical underpinnings in the field of special education in the 1960s when I began my informal studies firsthand within the family unit. My cousin Peter was diagnosed with autism when little was understood about the disorder. At that time, services were based on the beginning work of Bender (1964), Kanner (1943), Redl and Wineman (1957) and Rank (1949). As the field began to grow with research and reports from numerous case studies around the world by Rimland (1964), Schroeder, Mulick and Rojahn, (1980) and Lovaas (1977), I was introduced to the study of applied behavior analysis. Behavioral procedures, grounded in a scientific form of practice, attracted my interests at a time when critical information was sparse. Research in this field was demonstrating positive results in academic achievement and social domains. As the research addressed more diverse areas of societal concerns, and was synthesized by many including Sulzer-Azaroff and Mayer (1991), I realized how important it was to remain focused on environmental contingencies to be an effective teacher and leader. Clarity of purpose, well-formulated goals and objectives and a range of assessment tools to create a moving picture of change rather than a snapshot was a template of choice.

Within this context and theoretical framework, I began to identify the major elements that drive my work as an academic leader. Since this marks my thirtieth[h] year in the field of education, I will attempt to share reflections that began overlapping and emerging at every turn. Old journals were pulled from boxes and reread to create the story. The insights and lessons learned that I recorded along the way illustrate how I continue to strive to create an atmosphere that is more community-like, more democratic and more responsive to students pursuing a career in education and to serving the students and families with whom they come in contact within a wide range of urban settings.

The driving force behind my willingness to serve as an academic leader was a hunger to build bridges connecting School of Education (SOE) faculty, their school partners, the Liberal Arts and Science faculty, and the public, in more meaningful ways. I believed that a deeper understanding of our work was possible with our extended communities if we clearly articulated a vision and mission. This was no easy task, due to existing tensions in the School of Education. There were multidimensional and competing visions and missions that were driven by both external and internal forces. Shen (1999) writes about the tensions between the academic model, which heavily emphasizes scholarly production based on empirical research; the professional school model, which is often field based and pedagogical; and the reward system for tenure and promotion in a comprehensive university. This reward system is often in direct conflict with many stakeholders' (e.g., parents of students in our schools) expectations of SOE. They are less concerned with professors doing research, and more concerned with their pedagogy. They expect the preparation of teachers to meet the "high-quality standards" necessary for children to be competitive in the twenty-first century. In 1990, Boyer noted that faculty in Schools of Education are asked to embrace more and a wider range of missions. The profile of a professor of education is not clearly understood by administrators or colleagues outside of the SOE; they do not understand its depth, breadth and enormous need for clinical and field-based responsibilities. Moreover, these expectations vary depending on the local needs of the educational community in which they were situated. These important issues create additional challenges for a dean who must champion the work of faculty in a SOE.

There existed another challenge as well, as a special educator coming to higher education from the public schools: I came with a particular orientation. My vision was embedded in the belief that in order to prepare the most highly qualified educators, one had to be directly involved in schools, physically present and working alongside our P-12 colleagues. Not only would this allow us to generate more meaningful research questions, but we would also increase the probability that our research would inform practice. If equity and trust truly existed there would be a deeper relationship between theory and practice.

A balancing act is necessary. Our collectively developed mission statement is central to our identity as faculty members in a SOE, positioned within a larger college and university setting. If we agree on who we are and what our primary tasks are, then competing tensions could possibly ease and an opportunity for balance could exist between the diverse internal requirements and missions, as well as external expectations. Our research would have to be aligned with our shared vision and mission and would serve the purpose of improving the education of educators and show a collateral effect on P-12 renewal efforts (Gmelch, 2002). In addition, for our teaching and work in schools to be valued, that work would need to be aligned with our mission statement and reflect our beliefs our work was important and furthermore that we needed to embrace the moral responsibility to prepare educators for our nation's children (Goodlad, 1990).

After reviewing previous writings on developing and supporting school-university partnerships (Osguthorpe, Harris, Harris & Black, 1995), leadership in complex and chaotic times (Fullan, 2001), creating coalitions on behalf of our children (Senge, 2000) and the role of cooperation rather than competition (Kolodny, 1998), I presented the idea of revisiting the mission statement in light of the vision I presented to the faculty during the interview process and at the first SOE meeting. This endeavor was necessary in light of identified different philosophies and perspectives, different values, different turfs to defend and different agendas (spoken and unspoken). Barriers to change had to be confronted and adequate time and space created for significant ideas and understandings to emerge. There was a recognition that different faculty brought a variety of areas of expertise to the conversation and we would allow for permanent or rotating leadership in agreed-upon areas to occur—collaboration, critical self-reflection, diversity and social justice. My role as dean was to facilitate the larger conversation but encourage volunteers to provide team leadership in each of the identified areas including how the team monitored its own functioning. A climate of trust was created; conflict of ideas was managed effectively and a mechanism was established to share their collective efforts back to the entire body, a process recommended by Lucas & Associates (2000). Written reports were shared prior to our monthly meetings, so faculty had the opportunity to share comments for consideration or to suggest additional readings if definitions were not clear or required a shared language.

The process of developing a renewed mission statement took an entire academic year which involved starting with the overall vision and the mission statements of the university and college. We continue to refine the initial and related outcomes we agreed upon and the best means to obtain them. With new members joining the SOE each year, it became necessary to remain flexible as new ideas came forward and attempts to "practice what we preach" informed our next steps. The most important lessons learned over the years through trial and error, sharing with other deans, and reading, were to address conflict rather than avoid it. As changes came forward and the importance to nurture and reinforce institutional traditions, cultural practices and other contributions that continues to enrich this community of professional education scholars we faced, rather than avoided, their challenges (Reinhartz & Beach, 2004; Short & Greer, 1997; Skinner, 1987).

A calendar hangs in my kitchen from the W. K. Kellogg Foundation and serves as a daily reminder of what it takes for a seed of a good idea to flourish. William C. Richardson, president of the Foundation states:

> First, it must take root in the imagination of either an individual or a group of like-minded people. But after this initial growth, something larger must occur. Good ideas must be transplanted, as it were, into broader society where an ever wider circle of people can claim them as their own.

This statement has taken on a new meaning for me as I have learned from so many how "to yield a harvest." The ability to bring faculty together, to listen to and embrace new ideas lies at the heart of social change and is reflected in our mission statement. I've learned from mistakes as well as small and large victories as a dean and as a teacher prepared to be a special educator. I've outlined seven specific reflections below for consideration as you lead others forward.

Shared Vision

As special educators we believe in our hearts, as well as our minds, that we are prepared to deliver "special" services to "special" children and youth. Whether the task is academic, social, emotional, recreational, etc., we have the "right stuff." We embrace the notion that we can make a difference if given a chance, support and adequate resources. We have a passionate desire to provide educational experiences within academically rich and emotionally nurturing classrooms—across the school—to increase the probability that "our" students will be successful as well as accepted for who they are as individuals and members of the communities in which they reside. The civil rights movement, following decades of struggle, was critical in paving the way for our work to thrive and to achieve equity and excellence for all children. The struggle continues as we address issues of overrepresentation of black and Latino students; access to appropriate general education curriculum and highly qualified teachers. There was a sense of a clear vision and mission in the work of the School of Education and its faculty members, and as dean, I too, had to uphold that vision. These conversations, which I knew from my "teaching sense," involved the faculty playing an enormous role in contributing to the vision and in defining the ways in which they would be involved. This included involvement in schools (alone or with a team of colleagues). The process of building a learning community of people across disciplines and programs would be critical in sustaining our efforts. One person's vision does not allow for sustainability to occur.

The Role of Values

Discovering the challenges and complexities of bringing faculty members with competing beliefs and values together was deep and profound. I knew strong winds were blowing from external forces that were highly political and these same forces were seeking massive changes in the way we educated and prepared educators. In addition, tough economic times, new competitive pressures and often instability in leadership due to retirements and other environmental variables were challenging us.

Again, the values and beliefs developed in my previous work were resurfacing. A democratic classroom, now a SOE, cannot work if it's every person for himself or herself. As SOE faculty, we had nothing to lose and everything to gain if we celebrated our diversity of ideas and searched for our common beliefs and values. Was it possible to break down silos and build shared space? What is the purpose of public schooling? And how can colleges and universities partner with schools to ensure an educated citizenry capable of wise self-governance? Leading by consent, not by demand, takes longer and is harder, but allows everyone to come out a winner. Respecting each other's values and beliefs can be framed in this timeless advice.

The Plan

Whether in my first teaching assignment with the Dade County Public Schools in Miami or as a camp counselor, the need for a well-thought-out plan was important to stay focused on what had been identified as critical to the teaching and learning process. In public schools, the Individualized Education Plan (IEP), was an opportunity to structure the planning process as well as ensure that there be documented evidence that the plans were reviewed periodically with family and other members of the educational team. I had practiced writing IEPs as a special education teacher, and taught their importance and components to potential special educators as a professor. This, mandated by law provision, was a good base for me to move forward with my faculty as a dean.

As I approached the deanship, the idea of planning and writing the plan down was a form of not only critical self-reflection but also public reflection. Where are we today and where do we want to be at this time next year? In our current practices we call these things setting performance goals, outcome-based assessment and strategic planning. It is an easy transition for those deans with special education backgrounds. We have been doing this since the start of our careers. We valued the notion of documenting evidence of one's work to build upon, improve, enrich and/or eliminate practices that are not achieving mutually agreed-upon goals.

Strengths

From the beginning, my college professors in the special education program emphasized the positive. The rallying cry was "What can he/she do?" I continue this practice as a dean. If it is not apparent to me at first glance at their portfolio, I have faculty identify their strengths to assist in our efforts to realize our shared mission and implement our conceptual framework. They have wonderful ideas about how they fit into the whole—I remember to ask. In shared conversations, it has always amazed me how much is accomplished and how willing people are to work toward a common purpose.

The Power of Reinforcement

The most important skill I mastered is applying the principles of reinforcement. I observe behaviors closely and contingently reward colleagues for their accomplishments. Email has provided an immediate tool to recognize good work. With large numbers of faculty, it creates a mechanism to extend the communication system and use it for creating positive professional environments that value progress toward the shared goals aligned with our shared mission. Traditionally, the first SOE meeting starts with a summary of all the published work by faculty, grants received, awards won, presentations made at conferences as well as invited papers. Public recognition reinforces the concept that we have created a space to honor the distinguished work of each other and value the opportunity to share in the celebration.

Teaching and Learning

Special education is characterized by its focus on teaching (instructional practices) and student learning. We spend hours developing ways to differentiate small- and large-group instruction across the curriculum, evaluating our instruction frequently in terms of student performance and revising our work accordingly.

It was not surprising when the conversations in higher education shifted from merely those focused on pedagogy of higher education to the relationship between teaching and learning. This has created another wonderful opportunity for continuous shared interactions between faculty that are teaching the same sections, within the same program, similar topics across programs, or with their students themselves. Senge (2000) draws attention to his belief that colleges and universities "have become the preeminent knowing institutions in a world that increasingly favors learning institutions." (p. 129)

This challenging statement about the academy allows for this vital dialogue to be led by the faculty in Schools of Education. Change is happening all around us at an accelerated pace. My background suggests it will not help that we ride the winds of change but rather that we must seize the opportunity to go deeper into the research and complexities of the teaching and learning process. As Dean my job is to allow and promote the faculty to take ownership of the possible changes we seek to make in order to promote effective teaching and student learning.

Empowering Others

As a dean with a Governance Plan that supports empowering faculty, it was somewhat easier to get faculty to serve as members and assume leadership roles on committees, task forces, advisory boards and other organized groups around the campus where policy and practice is determined. I have discovered that if the work is aligned with the shared vision, mission and our conceptual framework, that empowerment comes naturally. Faculty step up to create ideas, invent what the future of the SOE will be, instead of trying to redesign past practices that are out of step with current renewal efforts.

Past experiences have shaped who I am today and the rewards of being a change agent have been powerful! The hard work, the long hours, the conflicting agendas, and local and public demands keep me focused on the primary shared vision, mission and conceptual frameworks that have been embraced and the documented evidence that they are all making a difference with those that matter the most—our students and the students and their families they serve. The development of "our students' capacities to create socially just, intellectually vital, aesthetically rich and compassionate communities that value equity and excellence, access and rigor," is what our mission is all about. As Speaker of the House Tip O'Neill said, "You can accomplish anything if you're willing to let someone else take the credit." This advice is visible and timeless, and both humble and empower me as a dean.

References

Bender, L. (1964). A twenty-five year view of therapeutic results. In P. H. Hoch & J. Zubin (Eds.). *The evaluation of psychiatric treatment* (129-142). New York: Grune & Stratton.

Boyer, E. L. (1990). *Scholarship reconsidered: Priorities of the professoriate.* Princeton, NJ: The Carnegie Foundation for the Advancement of Teaching.

Fullan, M. (2001). *Changing forces: The sequel.* London: Falmer Press.

Gmelch, W. H. (Ed.) (2002). *Deans' balancing acts: Education leaders and the challenges they face.* Washington, DC: AACTE Publications.

Goodlad, J. I. (1990). *Teachers for our nation's schools.* San Francisco: Jossey-Bass.

Kanner, L. (1943). Autistic disturbance of affective contact. *Nervous Child, 2,* 217-250.

Kolodny, A. (1998). *Failing the future: A dean looks at higher education in the twenty-first century.* Durham, NC: Duke University Press.

Lovaas, I. O. (1977). *The autistic child: Language development.* New York: John Wiley.

Lucas, A. & Associates (2000). *Leading academic change: Essential roles for department chairs.* San Francisco: Jossey-Bass.

Osguthorpe, R. T., R. C. Harris, M. F. Harris & S. Black (Eds.) (1995). *Partner schools: Centers for educational renewal.* San Francisco: Jossey-Bass.

Rank, B. (1949). Adaption of the psychoanalytic technique for the treatment of young children with atypical development. *American Journal of Orthopsychiatry, 19,* 130-139.

Redl, F. & D. Wineman (1957). *The aggressive child.* New York: Free Press.

Reinhartz, J. & D. M. Beach (2004). *Educational leadership: Changing schools, changing roles.* Boston: Pearson Education.

Rimland, B. (1964). *Infantile autism.* New York: Appleton-Century-Crofts.

Rutter, M. (1970). Autism: educational issues. *Special Education, 59,* 6-10.

Schroeder, S. R., J. A. Mulick & J. Rojahn (1980). The definition taxonomy, epidemiology, and ecology of self-injurious behavior. *Journal of Autism and Developmental Disorders, 10,* 417-432.

Senge, P. M. (2000). *Schools that learn: A fifth discipline field book for educators, parents, and everyone who cares about education.* New York: Doubleday.

Shen, J. (1999). *The school of education: Its mission, faculty and reward structure.* New York: Peter Lang.

Short, P. M. & J. T. Greer (1997). *Leadership in empowered schools: Themes from Innovative Efforts.* Upper Saddle Ridge, NJ: Pearson Education.

Skinner, B. F. (1987). *Upon further reflection.* Englewood Cliffs, NJ: Prentice-Hall.

Sulzer-Azaroff, B. & G. R. Mayer (1991). *Behavior analysis for lasting change.* Orlando, FL: Holt, Rinehart & Winston.

CHAPTER SIX

Leading from the Middle:
The Special Education Advantage

KATHLEEN MCSORLEY AND LEE ANN TRUESDELL

What qualities, skills, understandings and attitudes do special educators bring to the administrator's role? This is the question we attempt to answer in this chapter. We are both special educators who have been serving as assistant or associate deans of education at two campuses of the City University of New York for the past several years. Each of our large education units prepares hundreds of teachers, administrators, counselors and school psychologists for urban, culturally diverse schools. A significant part of our responsibilities focused on providing leadership for extensive educational change efforts including preparations for initial National Council for the Accreditation of Teacher Education (NCATE) accreditation. The purpose of this chapter is to delineate the qualities, skills, understandings and attitudes that we, as special educators, brought to the administrative roles of assistant or associate dean and how those qualities were used to provide leadership and facilitate faculty in responding to changes mandated by the state, city school system and university. It occurred to us that we called upon our special education backgrounds in various ways as we worked with faculty, administrators, school and state representatives to respond to various change initiatives. We often found ourselves "in the middle" with much responsibility, yet without the formal authority to garner necessary resources. We examine here what we brought to these roles; what we did to bring faculty together to work on tasks and how we facilitated completing the work.

Prior to assuming the roles of administrators, we were both members of the special education faculty. Prior to college teaching, we had been teachers of children with disabilities. As special educators, we developed many skills that we brought to our administrative roles, including setting and attaining goals, communicating and building relationships, interpreting regulations and guidelines, assessing performance, structuring tasks, and supporting learning and performance. We had also conducted staff development activities on a range of topics related to special education where we applied our skills as special educators to working with adults. We both had experience with school wide restructuring initiatives working closely with public schools to prepare teachers for the changes indicated in federal and state law and regulations, e.g., the Individuals with Disabilities Act (IDEA), with regard to educating children with disabilities.

We work in a very large public urban university at two different campuses with extensive educator preparation programs producing more than a thousand graduates each year. Our faculties are committed to preparing teachers and other educators to work in schools serving a culturally and linguistically diverse population and children with disabilities in inclusive and special settings. During our tenure as assistant and associate deans, the university directed all education units to prepare for NCATE accreditation. This decision followed three years of program revisions to meet new state regulations for teacher education certification. At the same time, the public school system launched an extensive teacher recruitment program that required the design and implementation of alternative teacher education programs for hundreds of new teachers. As special educators, mandates were not new for us. We had worked in special education during the years of great change resulting from Public Law 94–142 and IDEA. Thus, we were well equipped to interpret new regulations for teacher certification and accreditation requirements for faculty and other administrators. Furthermore, as special educators we brought a number of skills to the processes we used to facilitate a campus-wide response to the new state regulations for teacher certification and NCATE accreditation.

This chapter discusses three important aspects of our work as middle-level deans. "Functioning in the Middle" describes how we as assistant or associate deans worked closely with the deans, chairs and faculty to carry out the mandated program changes, accreditation efforts, school-based initiatives, as well as how we responded to school-based initiatives and institutional administrative tasks. "Setting and Attaining Goals" describes the overarching activity that organized so much of our work. As middle-level deans, we found ourselves translating regulations and mandates into goals and then establishing structures, scaffolds and supports for working toward and attaining the goals. Periodically, we reflected on the work and examined our strategies in a meta-analytic way to affirm or redirect faculty efforts. "Communication and Building Relationships" describes the critical role that communication and relationships played in building bridges, forging connections and creating learning communities. We attended to those who were marginalized and included everyone with a role to play and something to contribute. We used the critical special education practices of assessment, "meeting people where they were" and providing supports to those who asked to assistance. We found that the "label" of assistant or associate dean generated certain expectations among faculty and that, while we had little authority, we influenced the direction and outcomes of our education units.

Functioning in the Middle

Both authors experienced challenges and opportunities in their roles as middle-level deans within the hierarchical structure of the academy. The "labels" of assistant and associate clearly delineated our responsibilities within the unit as well as denoting a particular status position within our units and respective colleges. From the onset it was clear that we had very little formal power and authority to set policy and procedures, a situation we did not necessarily view as an obstacle in that we both believed that the accreditation process should be driven by faculty in alignment with our units' missions and conceptual frameworks. Yet we wanted very much to have a voice in the process and the outcomes. Like special educators so accustomed to working within interdisciplinary teams, the label of special education teacher served to identify our expertise within the team, not our status. Taking this perspective into our deans' roles we sidestepped the lack of formal authority to focus our energy onto creating influence and becoming change agents. One pathway to these outcomes was to work as participant observers in meetings and other open forums where we expressed our opinions and perspectives on issues and problems, while observing our colleagues in action. We had daily contact with students, contact that allowed us access to their issues and challenges. A benefit of this way of acting was that we became participants in the messy complexities of our organizations, revealing much about structural problems and cultural norms. While our titles positioned us in a hierarchy, our way of working flattened the structure to allow us to see and feel many issues from faculty as well as student perspectives and to advocate for change. We were truly in the middle, in the midst of so much activity and flow of information and ideas. This teaming, in a sense, built our credibility with colleagues and students. It also allowed us to communicate with our deans using primary-source data and information. While all parts of the organization did not function smoothly, the interdependence within our organizations became absolutely clear.

Senge (1994) speaks about the importance of systems thinking, the work of giving constant attention to the whole along with an analysis of whether its parts are, indeed, interdependent and interconnected. Costa and Kallick (1995) state that while we often think of boundaries as ways of defining turf, "systems thinking" highlights the relationships among bounded groups. Special educators are keenly aware of this as they work with families, other educators and service providers. And so, what better place to be than in the middle of such a mix to pose essential questions about interconnectedness and interdependence? We worked with our deans, our colleagues within our unit and in our Liberal Arts and Sciences departments and with our external constituencies of alumni and school partners to examine together the processes that bound us together. These included decision-making, priority setting, resource management, initiation of new practices and how disciplines worked together. And so our sphere of influence became this conceptual understanding and experience with interdisciplinary teaming. We created opportunities for ourselves to lead in this way. We took initiative and we took risks in asking these questions, for the integrity of the whole organization was examined for how its practices and purposes and culture aligned with the preparation of teachers. As the work of special educators is to advocate for equity and access for all students with disabilities, we saw it as our responsibility as middle-level deans to advocate for our students and faculty; we expected no less for ourselves in this new role.

Setting and Attaining Goals

One of the key functions that we performed as middle-level deans of education was establishing long-term and intermediate goals for our various responsibilities. As special educators, we were familiar and comfortable with goal setting and this was a natural step for us in the planning and leadership process. Goal setting and attainment involved four processes: translating and interpreting state and NCATE mandates, creating structures for faculty and staff to accomplish the goals, creating scaffolds and supports to facilitate faculty work, and reflecting on the processes and outcomes including looking at the big picture as well as the work in progress.

Translating and Interpreting Regulations

Teacher education experienced extensive changes in New York State during our tenure as middle-level deans. The New York State Regents established new requirements for the certification of teachers and other professionals that required extensive changes in our programs. Teacher education programs throughout the state were required to revise their programs and submit program documents to the State Education Department that described the programs and their philosophical foundations, staffing patterns, and school-based experiences. We directed this program re-registration process in our roles as assistant or associate deans. In order to facilitate faculty in revising programs and preparing re-registration documents, we needed to translate and interpret the state's requirements by recasting the new regulations into pedagogical, theoretical and empirical constructs familiar to faculty. That is, we found ourselves explaining what the state required by using examples from well-known conceptual frameworks, adjusting the paradigm analogies for different perspectives. At the same time, the process of translation and interpretation involved task analysis. We delineated specific tasks to shape faculty responses to the state regulations. We analyzed the state's requirements and laid out a series of steps that faculty could use to respond to the state mandates. Finally, we created structures such as formatted documents for faculty to use to make their responses.

Similarly, leadership of the NCATE process required ongoing translation and interpretation of the requirements, recasting the expectations for accreditation into familiar constructs. Translation and interpretation was particularly salient for the NCATE assessment requirements. Our institutions had not formally and consistently assessed students' competencies as a unit-wide activity. Nor had we looked regularly and systematically at evidence to assess the quality of our programs. Because our education units needed extensive discussion about systematic assessment, we established goals for faculty to grapple with the design of assessments for their programs. To attain these goals, we organized faculty retreats that engaged faculty in program groups to write assessment plans for their programs.

Structures

Major program change activities such as re-registration and accreditation required that faculty work together to redesign programs, formulate assessments to evaluate their programs and assemble assessment plans across departments. We created structures, forums, and processes for faculty to meet and discuss necessary changes. Providing structures was familiar to us as special educators who often designed special learning structures for our students. To organize the accreditation response process, we created committee structures across departments and units that focused on specific tasks. We designed and facilitated retreats where faculty participated in structured activities to think through and design assessment plans and program changes. We facilitated structured committee meetings where faculty formulated standards for student performance and processes for college-school collaborations. Our special education backgrounds prepared us to identify the goals to be attained, and the structures that would support faculty in working toward the goals.

Leithwood and Prestine (2002) outline what educational leaders need to do to respond to standards-based reforms. Our educational units were responding to state and national standards-based reforms in teacher education. We operationalized Leithwood and Prestine's ideas by designing structured meetings and retreats as well as arranging informal discussions and individual sessions to inform faculty of the new regulations and NCATE expectations. We needed to catch folks' attention and overcome the inertia of faculty working in stable programs. We moved the work forward by providing key information, examples and models for faculty to use and by providing feedback and prompts, and indicated to faculty, for example, that the program components and assessments they already had in place could be used in program revisions and NCATE accreditation procedures. Furthermore, we provided faculty with the tools they needed to produce documents and instruments. As in special education, we found that when we organized and structured faculty tasks, they were more responsive. The more specific the tasks, the more their responses fulfilled the regulation or accreditation requirements.

One of the most important activities that we facilitated was faculty discussions or dialogues that lead to shared understandings or meanings (Sergiovanni, 1989). Faculty needed to think out loud together to develop conceptual frameworks for our units and determine the assessments that reflect the frameworks. Heretofore, our units, like most other schools or departments of education, were organized by program and faculty rarely met together to talk about unifying ideas or to develop consensus about issues that cut across programs. As middle-level deans, we organized working groups of faculty across programs and facilitated dialogue in which ideas and perspectives from across the unit were shared and used to build unifying frameworks. As the reader can imagine, these discussions were not easy, and we often needed to provide a structured process so that all voices were heard and ideas shared. Furman and Starratt (2002) explain the process of dialogue:

> Dialogue theory centers more on understanding than on decision-making and "best arguments" . . . dialogue is usually taken to mean that each person in a communicative space has the chance to openly express her or his thoughts and feelings, that these are received without argument or judgment, and that this process repeats until larger understandings are achieved within the space. (p. 119)

Clearly, the dialogues that faculty engaged in initiated organizational changes in our units as members of faculty from different programs listened to one another and found common ground. As Senge (1994) articulates, learning organizations are where people expand complex understandings, clarify and develop visions and develop and modify mental models. Our units were developing into learning organizations through the dialogic processes we facilitated in our efforts to build a common set of ideas for accreditation activities.

Scaffolds and Supports

Supports and scaffolds are critical features of special education pedagogy that teachers use to guide and promote student learning (Murphy, 2002). As special educators, we drew upon this pedagogical grounding in our work with faculty and chairs to conceptualize new programs, reconceptualize current programs and prepare program changes to respond to the new state regulations. We also supported faculty in accreditation preparations by clarifying understandings of regulations and what was expected by the state education department and NCATE, reviewing written documents and providing feedback, providing formatted disks for faculty to write program and evaluation components in a coherent way, breaking down tasks into manageable pieces, facilitating faculty committee meetings, providing summaries during and at the end of the meetings, and indicating the next tasks on which committees needed to focus. These scaffolds and supports helped faculty to complete intermediate tasks and final program changes and assessments.

We created supportive learning environments for faculty similar to those found in effective special education programs (Murray, 2002). A key mechanism for achieving a supportive learning environment is to strike a balance between creating support structures and maintaining sufficient open space for faculty (learners) to grow and develop in their understandings of what was needed to respond successfully to state and national professional teacher education standards. Senge (1994) indicates that effective leaders function as teachers when they foster learning.

Reflection and Mega-Analysis

As middle-level deans, we were responsible for facilitating large change efforts within our education units as well as carrying out the routine administrative tasks of assistant/associate deans. Unlike the routine administrative tasks typical of our roles, the change efforts required extensive planning, facilitation and support to faculty engaged in, for example, rewriting programs or designing and implementing assessments. We found it necessary to calibrate our work by looking closely at regulations and accreditation requirements and then look at the work of faculty committees, and then back at regulations. We shifted our focus back and forth from a close look at regulations and faculty work to the overall picture. We would step back periodically to see how the various components fit together. We also kept looking at our own facilitation and management of these large-scale change efforts in a meta-analytic way, examining our work for its effectiveness in reaching our goals. We kept journals of our work and used them to rethink strategies and revise approaches. Through reflective journal writing, one author realized that a key assessment committee was too large to be a working group and reorganized the group into smaller task groups. We also sought counsel from other respected professionals. In one case, a colleague helped one author to understand how a group develops through a series of phases into a fully functioning task group.

Setting and achieving goals occurred not only through the creation of structures and processes, but also by engaging in systematic communications and building relationships with faculty, chairs, deans and the wider college community. In the next section we describe how these factors facilitated institutional change.

Communication and Building Relationships

Our work experiences with students with disabilities, their families and, to a large extent, with general education teachers and administrators, prepared us well as middle-level deans for the intense work of communication during the accreditation process. Special educators have a great deal of experience working with people who hold strong feelings and beliefs about students with special needs, about appropriate services and about best practice. Judgments and decisions about students with disabilities, and often about inclusion, are sadly all too often based not on data and team decision making but on strongly held unchallenged personal assumptions and beliefs. We found that in the early stages of the accreditation process, many of our colleagues held assumptions and beliefs about NCATE, about "accreditation" and "standards" that were based to some extent on prior knowledge and experiences, but mostly on philosophical perspectives that set them at odds with an outcomes- and standards-based approach in the academy. Our roles as NCATE coordinators positioned us to a degree as the "messengers" of NCATE, and our initial communications with colleagues were met with strong emotions about and resistance to accreditation. The differences among faculty on both of our campuses were deep and tensions initially were quite high in meetings where NCATE was an agenda item. As seasoned special educators, our skins were tough enough not to take our colleagues' communication in a personal way; after all, advocates for students with disabilities and inclusion are familiar with resistance and strong perceptions. However, we understood the necessity of hearing each individual faculty member's concern to understand them first of all as individuals, and secondly to allow their voices to reveal aspects of our organizational cultures. Our work as middle-level deans centered around moving individuals and groups of faculty from intensely personal views to consensual and collaborative expressions of new core organizational beliefs about accreditation. Senge (1994) addresses the importance of mental models in the learning organization, those beliefs and assumptions that shape the work, the structure and the culture of organizations. A key question that he poses for leaders in learning organizations is "what action do leaders take to help people see the need to do something that they may disagree with or not have the skills to do something about?"

We both learned that we could not assume that our colleagues were skillful in performance-based teaching and learning, and therefore much of our communication took the form of needs assessment, finding out what colleagues needed in order to enhance their own learning and skill development. Workshops and professional development activities were designed in response to their needs. In turn, as colleagues' knowledge and skills developed, they became advocates for the process. The communication system expanded to include colleagues who began to speak openly about their assessment systems, the connections they were making between standards and outcomes and how their syllabi and approaches to courses were evolving based on their new knowledge and skills. Initial assumptions changed and our cultures began to change as well in that we began to have different conversations and different communication patterns. Communication focused not only on what we needed to do, but how it could be done. Consensus for the work and the process of accreditation slowly developed.

As middle-level deans, we also realized that external data would be needed in the communication process as leverage with colleagues who were not moving and who were content to hold onto their assumptions about, and resistance to, the process. As special educators we both understood the power of data to create dissonance between what we think and what we know based on information and feedback. For data to serve as a tool to influence change it needs to be seen as the steady collection of information that then can weave an interesting story over a given span of time. Data can lead to surprise and wonder, to questioning, and can become focal points for rich discussions, for assumption testing and for action in response to the unfolding story. An unfolding story requires communication about what should happen next and one of our primary purposes as middle-level deans working with committees and groups was not to direct the conversations but to bring faculty together long enough to work out next steps, that is, to create the unfolding story within each of our organizations. Data collection, especially data from our students, led to emerging pictures of programs and the unit that could not be ignored. Student data proved significant in moving groups of faculty in new directions and resolved the issue of student marginalization as agents of change that did exist on one of the author's campuses.

As middle-level deans who coordinated the accreditation process, we could not help but notice individuals who appeared to be marginalized from, or on the fringe of, the community that was beginning to emerge. Our appreciation for individual differences and experience with difference empowered us to want to find out what contributed to this situation. We both felt that we saw behaviors in the organization that the dean might not observe because of the interactions and conversations we were having with colleagues. We felt that an essential part of our work was to focus on communicating with these individuals about their participation and feelings of belonging to the emerging community. Because we did not have the authority to evaluate, "hire or fire" them, we learned a great deal about the patterns of relationship within our organizations. We spent a lot of time observing and listening to our colleagues and participating with them, side by side, in ways that a dean did not. We observed patterns of relationships that were based on the perceptions that colleagues held about one another as scholars or as teachers, perceptions that were often formed prior to the NCATE process. We saw group dynamics unfold based on these perceptions that hindered the communication process and the trust building among faculty that was needed to become a community. And quite simply we saw faculty who preferred to work alone or who were not skillful or comfortable working in group situations.

Relationship-building was also challenged by the reality of a steady stream of new faculty who needed to find their sense of belonging in organizational cultures that were fragmented, to some degree, by the structure of discrete programs and departments. And relationships were challenged by the fact that faculty were also deeply engaged with their teaching, service and scholarship activities so necessary for tenure and promotion, work that created tensions for many about whether to focus on individual goals versus group work that would serve the goal of unit accreditation. Nevertheless we both felt that our special education background prepared us well for this work because relationships are so central to the work of special educators. Special education is largely about building relationships with others, creating communities focused on strengths and the vision of what is possible when people work together. We noticed that the change process called for abilities and competencies not needed before the accreditation process began. And so we became very engaged in finding out the strengths and interests of colleagues in areas not prioritized in the tenure and promotion process. Uncovering strengths and interests is quite natural for special educators, indeed it is an essential step in building relationships with students with disabilities. As middle-level deans we were able to ask colleagues whether they wanted to contribute to the community, how much and in what ways without judging them or evaluating their responses. For example—we needed faculty who *enjoyed* working with data and who communicated extraordinarily well through the presentation of data to others. This ability became highly valued and allowed individuals in both of our organizations, which preferred to remain on the fringe, to fully contribute to their college's accreditation efforts. Perceptions about these colleagues actually changed in positive ways as a result of these new patterns of relationships and the contributions they made to the accreditation process.

Also, while many new faculties were "newcomers" to our organizations, some brought prior accreditation experience and an understanding of the importance of collaboration and cooperation among colleagues. This vision was important to share, especially with colleagues who were still resistant to the process. As middle-level deans we mentored new faculty, built relationships with them and helped them to understand the history of their new organizations. And as middle-level deans we were not the "authority," a position that allowed us to some extent to be just like every one of our colleagues, individuals in search of a way of belonging to the organization and making a contribution. We believe this enabled trust to develop, and our invitations to colleagues to share their strengths and experiences with others were never turned down. We facilitated many committees that cut across programs and departments, decreasing fragmentation so that new faculty as well as seasoned faculty participated and learned much about each other and the organization. Committee work did not ease the burden of promotion and tenure activities, yet committees did generate the sense of working toward a common purpose, as near as we could get to a vision.

Conclusion

And so, we brought a resiliency to our work as middle-level deans because so much of what we saw and were asked to do corresponded to our work in special education. We laughed together while talking about this chapter, saying that we had been through greater challenges as special educators in large urban and public school systems than as deans. The notion that special educators have extraordinary patience seems to be true, for that characteristic proved to be helpful to both of us. We did not mind having to do and say things over and over, breaking the work down into little pieces, for eventually we saw the patterns connecting and a whole picture emerging. We both agreed that we were deeply optimistic and hopeful, true dispositions of special educators that carried us through the accreditation process. And we understood that influence is just as important as, or perhaps more than, authority in helping to create environments where relationships with others, creating community and achieving goals all are intertwined. That is what special educators know and do.

References

Costa, A. & B. Kallick (1995). Systems Thinking: Interactive Assessment in Holonomous Organizations. In A. L. Costa & B. Kallick (Eds.). *Assessment in the Learning Organization: Shifting the Paradigm,* Alexandria, VA: Association for Supervision and Curriculum Development.

Furman, G. C. & R. J. Starratt (2002). Leadership for democratic community in schools. In J. Murphy (Ed.), *The educational leadership challenge: Redefining leadership for the 21st century* (105-133). *One-Hundred-First Yearbook of the National Society for the Study of Education.* Chicago: University of Chicago Press.

Leithwood, K. & N. Prestine (2002). Unpacking the challenges of leadership at the school and district level. In J. Murphy (Ed.), *The educational leadership challenge: Redefining leadership for the 21st century* (42-64). *One-Hundred-First Yearbook of the National Society for the Study of Education.* Chicago: University of Chicago Press.

Murphy, J. (2002). Reculturing the profession of educational leadership: New blueprints. In J. Murphy (Ed.), *The educational leadership challenge: Redefining leadership for the 21st century* (65-78). *One-hundred-First Yearbook of the National Society for the Study of Education.* Chicago: University of Chicago Press.

Murray, C. (2002). Supportive teacher-student relationships: Promoting the social and emotional health of early adolescents with high-incidence disabilities. *Childhood Education, 78, 285-290.*

Senge, P. M. (1994). *The fifth discipline: The art and practice of the learning organization.* New York: Doubleday.

Sergiovanni, T. J. (1989). Value-driven schools: The amoeba theory. In H. J. Walberg & J. J. Lane (Eds.), *Organizing for learning: Toward the 21st century* (31-40). Reston, VA: National Association of Secondary School Principals.

CHAPTER SEVEN

Forging Leadership Approaches: Career Transitions for Two Women in Federal Service

SUZANNE M. MARTIN AND JANE M. WILLIAMS

The development of a person's leadership beliefs and practices usually is a cumulative process that occurs over the span of a career. Ideally, as we have new experiences within varying contexts, we evolve our thinking and actions based largely on the degree of success or lack of success we perceive we've had in using particular leadership strategies. Often our views of effective leadership are most strongly influenced by key transition points in our careers that cause us to reexamine the basic precepts of leadership that have guided us previously. The experiences we have and the lessons we learn during these transitions can help us forge a more expansive repertoire of knowledge, skills and attitudes about effective leadership that can serve us well in a wider variety of contexts.

In this chapter we will examine the experiences and lessons learned in one such key career transition that we shared. Coming from successful careers as educators in K–12 education and higher education, and as leaders in our professional organizations, we each chose to accept positions with the U.S. Department of Education (ED) in Washington, D.C. We would both be working in the Office of Special Education Programs (OSEP), a Division of the Office of Special Education and Rehabilitative Services (OSERS). (One of our earliest lessons learned was that you cannot escape acronyms in Washington!) While we had been colleagues previously through volunteer work with our primary professional organization, the Council for Exceptional Children, neither knew that the other was moving to the federal government. It was with considerable delight that we bumped into one another in our early days at the department and we became close colleagues and good friends over the course of our time in Washington. We shared many of the same beliefs, expectations, questions and concerns about our new positions and the leadership potential for each of us. As it turned out, our service in the department had a profound effect on our views of leadership and what type of leadership roles we would seek while with the department. Moreover, our federal service had a great influence on our decisions about what we would do professionally after we left the department.

While we are well aware that one cannot make generalizations from the experiences of just two persons, we do believe that the transitions we made into and out of the federal government were in many ways typical of others with whom we have spoken who worked at the U.S. Department of Education at some point in their professional careers. Hopefully, the reader will gain insights into the key role that such transitions can play and, more specifically, the impact of the leadership challenges and opportunities we encountered while at the department.

Our Pathways

Each of us came to the federal government with our own set of expectations based on what we thought we knew about how bureaucratic organizations function. Both of us had held a variety of professional roles in schools and higher education institutions and been actively involved at the local, state and national levels in leadership roles with our principal professional organization, the Council for Exceptional Children (CEC). We considered ourselves knowledgeable about the substance of the work related to the needs of exceptional individuals and relatively savvy about the politics of educational practice and policy in our field. We both had very positive views of the potential of education in the development of all students and the strengthening of society, but we felt also that we were attuned to the great difficulty of realizing that potential within the many constraints facing education today. We had worked in and managed improvement efforts of varying magnitude and had learned the importance of recognizing and respecting diverse views and building highly collaborative strategies to achieve desired ends. Each of us greatly enjoyed taking on new challenges and bringing together a wide range of people and interests to define and work toward a common cause.

How did we arrive at this crossroads in our careers at the same time? Our pathways to civil service at the federal level were similar, yet different. As mentioned earlier, we had known each other for several years in our respective leadership roles in CEC, the largest international professional organization dedicated to improving educational outcomes for individuals with exceptionalities, students with disabilities, and the gifted. We were both strong advocates for leadership through service, as evidenced by more than twenty-five years of CEC involvement for each of us. Initially, our work with CEC began as an attempt to learn more about children with disabilities and to apply that knowledge to our instructional practices in the classroom. Living in different parts of the country, we joined our respective local chapters and state federations of the CEC. We were both heavily involved in volunteer work on projects as well as extensive service on a wide variety of policy and practice committees. Each of us was subsequently elected to CEC offices at the local and state levels.

It is worth noting that our career paths as professional women prior to federal service reflected both historical and current trends for women. From one perspective, we both married young, and early decisions about our professional lives were often strongly influenced if not determined by the career opportunities of our spouses rather than our own. From another perspective, we were preparing ourselves for self-sufficiency by getting graduate degrees and developing our own profiles as respected professionals and leaders. Neither of us had children, allowing more time for professional pursuits. When life changes presented themselves in the form of divorce and later remarriage for each of us, we were prepared to address those changes from strong personal and professional foundations. Our life paths were not dissimilar from those of many other women of our generation. Our paths to leadership roles were perhaps more circuitous than linear, in part because of relocations according to our spouses' priorities and not ours. Yet the changing times provided us with many wonderful models of strong, independent women who were successfully balancing the many demands of their personal and professional lives. We had both been required to adapt and adjust significantly many times, but those experiences left us stronger, more fulfilled and happier in all dimensions of our personal and professional lives. It was with an optimistic outlook and abundant energy that we ventured forth to the wonders of Washington, D.C.

Life in the U.S. Department of Education

After our initial meeting in OSEP, we quickly discovered that we shared many questions about how our new positions would be different from our prior roles and how what we had learned to that point would relate to what we now faced. What would be the similarities and differences between the U.S. Department of Education's bureaucracy and what we had experienced previously? How could we quickly accomplish an environmental scan of the organization that would give us as much information as possible about how to navigate the system? How could we use this information to set one's compass in the right direction and make course corrections as we learned more? In addition to the skills and knowledge that we would need to do our jobs, to what extent would political issues influence our work and how would we maintain our ethical and moral focus within that context? Could we balance our professional goals and our professional integrity within a massive bureaucracy? Could we continue and strengthen our roles as national leaders in our profession now that we were part of the federal government? Could we further enhance our leadership skills and potential in our new roles? Were there unique challenges that we would face as women in an organization reputed to have mostly male decision makers? Finally, and most critically, how could we ensure that everything we did would eventually contribute to providing the best possible education for our target population, all of those individuals with exceptional needs?

Many of these questions derived from some ambivalence about working at the federal level. On one hand, the possibility of having a greater impact on a grander scale was seductive. We both had been involved in many situations where we'd had success on a smaller scale and knew that we should be sharing this information with others facing the same issues. But there was rarely time, money or appropriate connections to reach out so we remained focused only at the local level. At the federal level we hoped to have the chance to look across improvement efforts nationally, analyze lessons learned and make this knowledge available to others in similar situations to inform decision making and to avoid reinventing the wheel.

On the other hand, we knew the reputation that the federal government had among many education practitioners and policy makers. Many felt that ED's contributions were limited in improving education and that federal efforts were often counterproductive due to the many regulations and extensive reporting and record-keeping requirements that usually went along with federal involvement. Many educators felt that federal bureaucrats were uninformed and out of touch with local and state needs. Yet we knew that this was only one part of the picture. Both of us had worked in federally funded projects that had been essential in improving practice. We and our colleagues knew many federal employees whose knowledge and support had been instrumental in helping us accomplish our goals at the local and state levels. Those employees were the ones we hoped to emulate. We firmly believed that the potential contributions from the federal level were great and we were determined to play as positive a role as possible.

In the four years that Dr. Martin spent at OSEP and the five years that Dr. Williams spent there they had diverse responsibilities. Dr. Martin was located in the Research to Practice Division where she began as an Education Program Specialist and rose to the Acting Branch Chief for Personnel Preparation. Under her guidance was the funding of preparation programs for leaders in special education and for teachers of students with serious emotional disturbances. She was also responsible for oversight of funding for projects of national significance in special education. Her duties included budgetary planning, program review and supervision of branch personnel.

Two examples of situations that Dr. Martin faced in maintaining and expanding her leadership roles within OSEP as well as nationally illustrate some of the obstacles she faced. Despite the fact that a primary reason for hiring Dr. Martin was her national profile as a recognized expert in her field, she was told as she began work that she would have to relinquish her membership on the CEC executive board. Eventually she was able to work through the ED system with the aid of colleagues and get a legal ruling that she could remain on the board as long as she was not involved in developing or making federal judgments about any proposal from the board. Later in her time at ED she had to pass on an opportunity to be on the ballot for the presidency of CEC due to possible perceptions of conflict of interest. It is understandable that issues of conflict of interest needed to be addressed but it is also a negative factor that potential federal employees must consider when seeking to maintain national leadership roles.

The second issue was related to the fact that during Dr. Martin's first two years of ED service there were four divisions within OSEP and branches within each division. After that time, OSEP was reorganized and comprised only two divisions with a reduced number of branches in each division and a team structure replacing many of those branches. Thus the promotion and leadership opportunities within OSEP were drastically reduced for both Dr. Martin and Dr. Williams. Dr. Martin has risen to acting branch chief, but her branch was eliminated in the reorganization and the two division director positions above her were already filled.

Dr. Williams spent four years in the Monitoring and State Improvement and Planning Division of OSEP and one year in the Research to Practice Division. As a program officer she served as the federal contact for numerous states and territories receiving monies through Part B of the Individuals with Disabilities Education Act (IDEA). Dr. Williams had an oversight role to ensure that these funds, allocated to states and territories based on the number of students with disabilities within their boundaries and considered entitlement dollars, were appropriately used to support the provisions of IDEA Part B. Her leadership skills were put to the test as she assisted state leadership personnel to ensure that implementation of IDEA was consistent with federal requirements and exemplary practices. Upon moving to the Research to Practice Division, she served as director of the Secondary, Transition and Postsecondary Team, providing budget oversight to support the development of systems and programs to implement services to students with disabilities at the secondary and postsecondary levels.

We both knew that whatever the obstacles, a key to expanding and strengthening our leadership skills and knowledge was to avail ourselves of opportunities for continuing, high-quality professional development. We each had intense demands in our new positions and it was difficult to find the time and locate the opportunities for such professional development. ED had many types of programs of study that were available to employees but the problem was to identify quality initiatives and find time to participate. We were both firm in our belief that quality professional development was not a piecemeal, one-shot event but a long-term process and commitment. We sought out and were chosen to participate in, for Dr. Williams, a two-year ongoing leadership training program and, for Dr. Martin, a two-year training program on accountability issues in educational leadership. We also volunteered to serve on several planning groups within OSEP and OSERS and across the department as learning and leadership opportunities. For example, Dr. Martin served for two years as the OSEP representative on the department's Professional Development Team, which worked to coordinate all the departmental efforts to award funds for professional development activities at the local and state levels.

Many educators at all levels of the system certainly can relate to the tensions between the need to improve continuously and the scarcity of time and quality programs in which to do so. Even though we felt we knew our field well, the diversity of activities with which we were involved across the nation demanded more wide-ranging and more in-depth knowledge and skills than we had previously acquired. We found ourselves always in a catch-up mode but were grateful for the learning opportunities wherever we could find them. The programs and seminars at the department did prove, in fact, to be well grounded in the realities of practice. The committee work was perhaps even more valuable. One has to build relationships and alliances within one's own program as well as with people across the entire department if the job is to be done well. You need to look for mentors and probe the depths of their knowledge and capitalize upon their willingness to help you navigate the system. It was also very important that we build upon each learning opportunity by seeking out the next logical progression of learning. If you are standing still, you are moving backward in relation to grasping the ever-expanding knowledge that exists today.

Another harsh reality for a program officer in the department is that you will not spend all of your time working on substantive issues. There is much substantive work to be done in developing competitions and working with funded projects, but there are also myriad regulatory, legal, reporting, compliance, scheduling and logistical issues that must be addressed as well. In our experience, as much as one-half of our time was spent on this latter set of issues. Federal service gives you the opportunity to work with experts around the country and to stay abreast of cutting-edge improvement efforts nationwide. Perhaps nowhere else can you have the access you have at the federal level to support high-quality work and help to develop needed linkages among those involved. The trade-off is the amount of time you will have to spend working on bureaucratic necessities that can drain your energies and detract from your time for more substantive interactions with the field. If you are considering federal service you need to realize that this is the nature of the beast and both types of activities are essential parts of the job.

The Impact on Our Beliefs about Leadership

Our new work contexts and our evolving roles as leaders within OSEP required us to closely examine our underlying beliefs about what really comprises effective leadership. For us, as in the literature, leadership is defined in numerous ways. Effective leadership is visionary yet practically grounded in the best available knowledge and practice. It is action oriented with mutually agreed-upon and clearly stated objectives, goals and strategies, and valid and feasible ways to assess progress and modify activities accordingly. It is results focused with emphasis on valid and reliable assessments of learner progress toward relevant and significant outcomes. Effective leadership knows how to bring together, maintain and expand the human, financial and other resources that will be necessary to ensure progress and overcome obstacles. It is doing what is best, not necessarily easiest or safest, for the target populations—in this case, individuals with exceptional needs and all those who influence their development. In many instances it is, to paraphrase Eleanor Roosevelt's words, "doing what you think you cannot do" (1960, p. 54).

Perhaps the most difficult aspect of our leadership roles within OSEP was continuously developing and effectively using the full extent of our cognitive abilities, insights and sensibilities to define and pursue a vision that would be clearly understood and widely supported by stakeholders in special education. Often the parameters of this vision were defined by congressional language and/or administration priorities and our task was to mesh these guidelines with the realities, needs and talents of those in the field. Many times this was a labor of love as the mandates were consistent with our beliefs, values, ethical and moral perceptions and professional knowledge and standards. However, at other times these mandates and priorities were in conflict with our own views. On some occasions the legislative or administration language was in draft form and we could sometimes work through the system to try to get the language changed to conform more closely to what we perceived to be the realities of the field. More often we were in a position of having to do our best with what we had received. That meant providing leadership in seeking what we perceived to be the best possible result for our target populations within the constraints of mandates which we personally felt were to some extent ill-formed or even misguided. To us this was the greatest test of our leadership capabilities and often resulted in much personal turmoil as we sought to reconcile personal views that were in conflict with organizational demands. We believe that we did the best we could to produce competitions and programs that were as responsive to the field as possible no matter whether we agreed with the initial mandate or not. But it is clear that leadership at the federal level, at least among mid-level program officers, can be a trying experience when such personal conflicts arise. With the ever-changing tide of congressional and administration priorities it is not surprising that many who enter federal service grow weary of the conflicts in a relatively short time and decide to get out of the water and move on in their careers.

Another priority in our leadership efforts was to maintain a clear focus on the shared goals of the government and those in the field. In our case, the principal shared goal was the provision of a free and appropriate public education for students with disabilities. We were constantly aware of Lewis Carroll's reminder in <u>Alice in Wonderland</u> that "If you don't know where you are going, any road will take you there" (p. 104). We needed to help states and our local grantees and contractors ensure that we were all using the same map. We needed to be clear that we were providing support to establish the infrastructure in states and recipients of discretionary monies to reach our shared goal of providing programs, services and supports that would achieve the desired outcomes of IDEA.

We believed that to do this a leader must be strategic, supporting and guiding his/her colleagues toward a shared goal that will maximize the result for our constituents. We saw our leadership role as helping constituents explore alternatives and decipher the best route or routes to maximize results. The crux of our leadership responsibilities was the difficult task of using our skills, knowledge and finesse to mesh the goals of constituents with those of the department. As leaders we needed to create a community of supporters at the federal level and in the field who would translate, reinforce and transform a shared vision into actions that would benefit all organizations involved. We believe that leadership is the key to organizational success (Brem, 2001).

We felt that the work of William Pearce was perhaps most relevant in thinking about how to mold our leadership beliefs and actions to fit our situations. Pearce (2001) discusses the hard work required for one to be a "soft manager." He elaborates by saying, "soft management does not mean weak management. It means candor, openness and vulnerability, but it also means hard choices and responsible follow-up" (p. 89). We believe that "soft qualities" such as sensibility and openness are as valuable as "hard qualities" such as charisma and aggressiveness when it comes to leadership.

At the federal level, as at many other levels, a person exhibiting soft leadership can be dismissed as a weak leader. Sensibility is often mistaken initially for "touchy-feely." Yet the benefits of being "soft"—e.g., being caring, open and sensitive—can bring many benefits. No matter what one's leadership style, people need to feel significant and rewarded for what they do. Leaders will be followed when they recognize and respect all stakeholders' work as having merit and contributing to the goals being pursued. Leaders will be rewarded with loyalty when they show the same willingness to learn and change as is expected of those with whom they work. A leader must be a model both of clarity of vision and of flexibility in seeking better ways to pursue that vision. These are the traits that will give meaning to a person's professional life and will result in a greater depth of shared ownership of the work that needs to be done. Both of us also found that this "soft" leadership style and a positive outlook were also very useful in maintaining high morale, especially in a large bureaucracy where the feeling of loss of individual identity was often rampant. Goleman, Boyatzis and McKee (2001) have found that a leader's mood has the greatest impact when it is upbeat, though his/her mood must also reflect the understanding of the dynamics of the situation.

The "soft" style of leadership is often associated with women, especially in the helping professions. Women far outnumber men in many of these professions, as is certainly the case in special education. Yet the effective use of the "soft" style often seems more related to the nature of the work being done, the context for that work, the type of people with whom the leader is working, and the leader's personality, than to the gender of the leader. Everyone does not always value, we quickly learned, "soft" leadership. We recognize that some of these "soft" traits that we exhibited were traits that some colleagues, women included, had worked hard to eliminate from their own leadership repertoire. It is our belief that, contrary to some opinions, "soft" leadership is not for the weak or timid. As much as any style, it means standing in the crossfire, accepting the consequences and risking being unpopular. A "soft" leader has to make the same hard decisions as any other leader. It is a matter of choosing a style that works for a particular person and a particular context.

We also believe that effective leaders are change agents who mentor others and who maintain broad, long-term networks of people who can be called upon for assistance in whatever efforts are being pursued. Both of us have had mentors of great importance throughout our careers and since our earliest professional years have developed and maintained wide networks of colleagues who are always available to help us examine what we are doing. Mentoring makes a difference. It helps with answers to questions and it helps provide stability, guidance, support, and affirmation through one's career. We both believe that future leaders inside and outside federal service need to be encouraged to maximize their potential, to explore the road to leadership, recognizing that the path may not be linear. We need to help young leaders establish contacts, networks of colleagues who will support them in their current position and in their next "stop" along the way. We need to help young leaders address the balance that is required between their professional and personal lives. We need to help young leaders learn how to protect and balance both their professional and personal lives, not take attacks or setbacks personally, and have a source of replenishment for their emotional energy. One who is empty or "burned out" will not be of any value to themselves, their colleagues, subordinates, or the organization. We need to help young leaders learn to navigate the professional world, which is often clouded by egos an personal agendas. We need to help young leaders see that one of the keys to leadership is to always be preparing and positioning oneself for the next career challenge—and always challenging themselves to "raise the bar." We also have a responsibility to stimulate and transfer to them a passion for our profession and our life's work. As Josaitis reminds us, "If you believe in something and have passion for it, you stand up for it. And you have to be persistent, no matter how long it takes" (Collingwood, 2001, p. 11).

Effective leaders must also have a commitment to excellence. While both of us had often heard the phrase "good enough for government work," in actuality, very few of our colleagues adhered to that standard. Most of our colleagues were striving for a higher standard in spite of obstacles they faced in the massive bureaucracy. One reality for leaders in such a setting is recognizing that rarely will excellence equate to perfection. When there are so many diverse political forces at work as there are in the federal government it is often the case that initiatives get watered down in order to mollify as many political views as possible. A leader still has to push for the best result possible and convince others that this is worth doing and the best contribution possible under the circumstances. Add to this the many roadblocks that one faces in addressing many of the other bureaucratic necessities mentioned earlier and you have the potential for a great deal of frustration among federal workers. Because frustrations can run high and a sense of personal accomplishment may be very fleeting, maintaining one's equilibrium as a leader in this situation is imperative.

Finally, we believe that true leaders possess a moral and ethical compass which guides their personal and professional integrity, and without which effective leadership is not possible. As Gilmartin affirms, "to have a healthy organization, you need leaders who conduct themselves ethically and treat people with dignity and respect" (Collingwood and Kirby, 2001, p. 54). Working in a large organization can be ethically challenging. The volume of the work alone would indicate a need for cutting corners. The isolation from your learning community in the sense of not having daily contact with your customers—students with disabilities and their families—can be numbing. The interactions with your colleagues in the external learning community and in the government can be confusing. Does the field respect me for the quality of my work, or are they just interested in the federal dollars? How do I reconcile my personal views with those of my organization when there are differences? What is the proper balance between my agency oversight role and my role as a professional colleague to those in the field? We were in the business of building public trust. We had to be above reproach. Understanding and heeding the concept of an "appear-

ance of impropriety" is challenging. Leadership in the face of these conflicts is
not easy. Pagonis (2001) refers to it as leadership in the combat zone. We decided early in our careers that high ethical and moral standards would always be
a major part of our professional lives. Our time with the government was both
a test and affirmation of the importance of those standards.

Lessons We Learned

We know that our experiences with OSEP were extraordinary. In some re-
spects, we wielded considerable influence. One of our greatest pleasures, upon
reflection, is that we truly believe we used our influence to better the lives of
large numbers of students with disabilities and their families. Specifically, what
did we learn? As we revisit the experience now, almost a decade later, and reflect upon our contributions, our insights, and our work, we leave you with a
few examples:

- Following one's professional, moral and ethical compass is possible
  within a large bureaucratic organization. While we sometimes struggled
  to do this, we persevered and succeeded. Our efforts, along with the
  extensive new knowledge, skills and competencies we accrued while at
  OSEP, have helped us gain additional respect from many of our peers
  and colleagues. We also recognized that we were spokespersons for the
  administration under which we served. Our responsibility to respect
  that relationship was compatible with maintaining our self-respect. Indeed, to have the responsibility for providing oversight—that is, to
  "monitor" our clients, and still maintain the respect of those with
  whom we had that relationship, is very rewarding. We must have done
  something right.
- Being prepared for opportunities is crucial. It was important that we
  had both had a range of successful experiences before we came to
  Washington. Equally important, perhaps, is that our federal experience
  prepared us for taking our careers to the next step. Both of us are now
  in higher education. Both of us have been able to build upon our experiences to move to positions of considerable importance to us and to
  our institutions. We gained immeasurable knowledge from working
  with the best in our field around the country and we are now applying
  much of what we learned. Through better teaching, new administrative-

level work, expanded networks of knowledgeable colleagues and national leadership roles in CEC we are better able to contribute meaningfully to our organizations and our profession.

- Maintaining your focus is crucial. We were able to stay focused, to remember that our position meant service to our stakeholders that would result in better results for students with disabilities and their families. We believe that we were able to marry our knowledge, skills and competencies with our personal and professional integrity while still keeping our eyes on the prize.

- Understand the system. We were able to navigate the system, use our knowledge and our skills to negotiate and achieve our goals through effective strategic planning. As one of our dear friends has said, "We were able to swim with the piranhas." We did not succumb to a large bureaucracy that had its own needs, but learned to work within that system while maintaining our values and ethics.

- Change is going to happen. The issue is whether it will be positive or negative. We were change agents. Many of our "products" are alive and well in today's schools benefiting our most important constituents—students with disabilities, and their families. We continue to serve as change agents, serving as role models, mentoring our students—teacher candidates and administrators-in-training, collaborating with our colleagues and providing national leadership for CEC.

- Be able to juggle and walk the balance beam. We were usually able to balance the needs of a large bureaucratic organization with our needs and the needs of our constituents clients, and stakeholders. Our clients were diverse—state education agency representatives, personnel from institutions of higher education, parents affiliated with parent training and information centers. Our responsibilities were many. We were by no means perfect but excellence was always our standard.

- Bring your style, grace and composure. We were able to execute our leadership styles within a bureaucratic environment successfully. We used our "soft" leadership style to effect change. We enjoyed our work and supported others to help them enjoy their work. We could work harmoniously within a large bureaucratic organization remembering that the laws, regulations, policies, procedures and practices had the potential to serve the infants, toddlers, children, youth and young adults with disabilities and their families. No hidden or personal agenda could be permitted to detract from that focus.

Summary

When Dr. Williams left the federal government and entered higher education, she focused on her teaching responsibilities but also perceived the need for her teacher candidates to be involved in their special education professional organization as one way of beginning to develop themselves as leaders. What better way to model this behavior, and solicit service from the teacher candidates, than to revive a defunct student chapter of CEC? She served as the student chapter adviser for her four years at that institution. She watched her students mature, learning the many lessons of professional and community involvement and reaping the rewards of dedicated service. Concurrently, she resumed her leadership role at the state level, serving as vice president and president of her state CEC federation. At present she serves at the national level as treasurer of CEC's Division on Career Development and Transition and is teaching again at the University of Nevada Las Vegas.

Dr. Martin moved back to higher education as well but decided to explore the potential of an administrative role. She served as a department chair in Special Education and then accepted a position as a professor in Special Education and an assistant dean of Administration and Accreditation at the University of Central Florida. Dr. Martin also continues to pursue her interest in the role of families in special education through grant projects. She was elected president of the CEC's Division of Teacher Education and subsequently was elected to the CEC presidency in 2004. While the demands of her dual roles are great, Dr. Martin serves as a model for what is possible when the support of those who recognize the multiple responsibilities of a true educational leader is available.

We have been fortunate to contribute to the programs, services and supports for many students with disabilities and their families through our work with the U.S. Department of Education. It was a marvelous experience and opportunity and we have reaped many benefits on a personal and professional level. We continue to cherish our higher education roles as well as our service to our professional organizations. We strive always to be agents of positive change and we hope that the next generation of leaders will consider federal service, benefit from the lessons we've learned and glean some helpful information from our journey. We heartily recommend federal service to anyone who is looking for a true learning experience and a great opportunity.

References

Brem, M. L. (2001). *The 7 greatest truths about successful women: How you can achieve financial independence, professional freedom and personal joy.* New York: Berkley Publishing Company.

Carroll, L. (1866). *Alice in Wonderland.* London: William Heinemann

Collingwood, H. (2001). Personal histories: Leaders remember moments and the people that shaped them. In *Harvard Business Review on Breakthrough Leadership*, Boston: Harvard Business School Publishing Corporation, 1-24.

Collingwood, H. & J. Kirby (2001). All in a day's work. In *Harvard Business Review on Breakthrough Leadership*, Boston: Harvard Business School Publishing Corporation 51-70.

Goleman, D., R. Boyatzis & A. McKee (2001). The hidden drive of great performance. In *Harvard Business Review on Breakthrough Leadership*, Boston: Harvard Business School Publishing Corporation, 25-50.

Pagonis, W. (2001). Leadership in the combat zone. In *Harvard Business Review on Breakthrough Leadership*, Boston: Harvard Business School Publishing Corporation, 105–126.

Pearce, W. (2001). The hard work of being a soft manager. In *Harvard Business Review on Breakthrough Leadership*, Boston: Harvard Business School Publishing Corporation, 89-103.

Roosevelt, E. (1960). *You Learn by Living.* New York: Harper and Brothers.

CHAPTER EIGHT

Promoting Faculty Diversity for Women and Minorities in Higher Education: Journeys and Challenges

VIVIAN I. CORREA AND PATRICIA ALVAREZ MCHATTON

One of the major concerns in institutions of higher education (IHE) across the country is the recruitment and retention of faculty from underrepresented groups. Many predominately white universities (PWU) face significant challenges when diversifying the faculty. The charge to increase diversity at most universities is typically viewed as increasing the numbers of African American, Hispanic, Asian, and Native American faculty. However, diversity in many disciplines also means increasing the number of women (e.g., in engineering) or men (e.g., in nursing) on the faculty. Furthermore, universities are mindful of the need to increase the numbers of persons with disabilities and protect the rights of faculty and staff who come from diverse religious backgrounds and diverse sexual orientations.

Departments of special education at many universities face multiple challenges related to diversity of the faculty. Not only are they lacking in the numbers of faculty from culturally and linguistically diverse backgrounds but they are also faced with a critical faculty shortage (Smith, Pion, Tyler & Gilmore, 2003). Much has been written about the plight of faculty members who are in the minority at predominately white universities (Garcia, 2000a; Moody, 2004; Padilla & Chavéz, 1995; Vargas, 2002). Some emphasis has also been placed on the challenges minority and females face in academia (Aguirre, 2000; Cooper & Stephens, 2002; Vargas, 2002). The purpose of this chapter is to present the challenges and critical issues facing special education faculty from diverse backgrounds as well as documenting the experiences of two Hispanic female faculty, one at a predominately white university and the other at an Other Minority Institution (OMI) serving at least 25 percent or greater minority population. Their narratives serve to illustrate the pathways, challenges and rewards they faced as Hispanic women. Then the chapter will (a) review the current status of faculty from diverse backgrounds in special education, (b) provide the rationale for increasing the numbers of diverse faculty[1] and (c) outline strategies for how diverse faculty can successfully navigate the challenges they may face at predominately white universities and OMIs.

Leadership is defined in many ways. One way to improve your status is to become educated. For women from diverse backgrounds, the rise to leadership positions, such as achieving a professoriate rank, has been slow in coming. We hope that this chapter will encourage female faculty of diverse backgrounds to move forward in academia, reaching their goals and serving as mentors for others who follow them.

Being the Only One:
Narrative from a Senior Faculty Member and Associate Dean

I never really thought much of being the only Hispanic in my undergraduate and graduate classes at Georgia State University, the University of Georgia and Vanderbilt University. My experiences seemed very "mainstream." I worked hard, struggled with writing, but believed everyone was having similar experiences. Although I had good relationships with the instructors in my classes, I had no Hispanic role models in college. I was socialized to be a special educator without regard to my own cultural and linguistic background. My Hispanic identity consisted, basically, of checking the boxes for Hispanic/Latino on applications and other forms. I spoke very little Spanish during my college years and practiced only a little when I visited my family. Now I realize that somewhere in the process of my K–12 and college education, I had lost my Puerto Rican identity and did not even realize it until later in my life. Had I assimilated to the "mainstream" and forgotten my roots?

My Latina consciousness wasn't really raised until I was hired as an assistant professor at the University of Florida (UF). Although I was the only one in my department, I was not the only one at the university. In 1990, I worked with five other Hispanic faculty to establish the first Association of Hispanic Faculty

---

[1] For the purposes of this chapter, diverse faculty are minorities, women and individuals with disabilities who traditionally have been underrepresented in higher education.

and Staff on campus. I served as the secretary of the association the first year and became president the second year. I learned very quickly that the visibility of being one of the only Hispanics on campus would take its toll on my time and commitment to university service. Thank goodness I had been tenured and promoted to associate professor the year before the service obligations began to roll in. Nonetheless, I still faced the challenge of working toward promotion to professor. My load on service far outweighed the load of my White, non-Hispanic colleagues. I realize, now, that I could have said no to the numerous invitations to serve on university committees, search committees and advisory councils of various organizations on campus. However, the message from the few Latino faculty on campus was that Latinos needed strong representation and that the voices of Latinos needed to be heard! For the first time, I felt an obligation to represent "my people." But at what expense?

My identity as a Latina was transformed dramatically through those years and the transformation continues today. Interestingly, the transformation also took place in my own research and teaching activities. I had come to UF to teach in the area of severe and multiple disabilities. During the early 1990s my research turned toward bilingual special education and working with Latino families. I designed and taught the various courses on multicultural education in early childhood special education, and was invited to write various chapters on the topic of culturally diverse students. I was promoted to professor in 1992, after one of the most stressful and productive periods in my career. I also credit my success of this milestone to the fact that I was single and had no children. I devoted 100 percent of my time in the evenings and on weekends to my work.

Although my productivity in research and teaching were strong, the service work continued to dominate my day-to-day life and extended to professional organizations as well. Even today, the invitations to serve in a leadership capacity are a struggle. I question the motives of people who ask me to join their committees, councils and boards. I often feel like the "token" on many of these committees—window-dressing for the university. Most groups are not blatant about the reason for my appointment to the committee. However, on one occasion, my term on the board was complete and I had asked if they needed help finding a replacement. The chairperson of the council said, "Yes, we need your help finding a replacement, but you know they must be Hispanic."

The joy associated with my achievements is often overshadowed by my fear that I achieved only because I was a woman and Hispanic. Unfortunately, my fear has been affirmed by a couple of "well-intentioned" colleagues who have said, "Congratulations on your accomplishment. It sure didn't hurt that you were Hispanic."

For the majority of my special education academic career, I have taught predominately White, female, middle-class, young adults. Until recently, I never saw students who were like me in my classes. However, with the increase of the Hispanic student population at the university, I have begun to experience the connection with Latino students. Now it is common to have at least one or two Hispanic, African American, or Asian students in class. Most gratifying has been my work mentoring Latina doctoral students, one of whom is my co-author! These young women will learn the successes and pitfalls they may face as new assistant professors at universities. I will nurture their cultural and linguistic identities, counsel them about resisting the silencing of their voices or masking of their identities, while at the same time guiding them through the realities of being the only one or one of the few at a predominately white university.

How have these experiences influenced who I am today? Some indicators are evident. I am speaking more Spanish! Each semester, when I meet my new students I introduce myself as being Puerto Rican and share with them some of my childhood experiences, academic achievements and continuing struggles as a minority woman. I am more confident and committed to helping the university community become more responsive to *all* students and faculty, including those from underrepresented groups. My latest accomplishment? Becoming associate dean of the Graduate School in charge of overseeing recruitment and retention programs for graduate students at the university.

Connecting to My Roots: Narrative from a New Assistant Professor

My family and I arrived in the United States in the early 1960s, after Castro's takeover in Cuba. Arriving here as a young child was somewhat disconcerting. Due to my father's work for an American-held company, he had been forced to leave the country clandestinely, leaving us behind until arrangements could be made for us to leave as well.

Upon arrival, both my sister and I spoke very little English. We were immediately enrolled in school in what would be considered full immersion. As time passed, I quickly became acculturated, as young children do, and rarely did I think of my birthplace. I was, after all, in America. I never fathomed the burning desire to reconnect to my roots that would awaken as time passed, fed by my experiences in life, agitated by my experiences in education.

I went on to work in a male-dominated field where I continued to see and hear discrimination beyond ethnicity. During this time of my life, with a young child to rear, I was less vocal. I decided to go back to school to become a teacher and work with all those students whom no one else wanted to work with. As I maneuvered my way through my undergraduate and graduate studies, I was faced with issues of diversity, hegemony, and disparate treatment and opportunity for students of color. In addition, in every class, or so it seemed, we were encouraged to "reflect" on our school experiences. The diversity issue confounded the meritocracy beliefs, and I had no desire to reflect on my school experiences. Having lived through them was painful enough; I felt no need to dredge them all up again.

It was not until I began doctoral studies that the enormity of this issue came to light. I spent two years undergoing a transformation. I had changed forever. I now yearned for connections to my roots. I looked around and found no one. Yes, I had some wonderful mentors, several of whom understood my journey, and one who I think in some ways understood it better than I did. It was through one of these mentors that I was encouraged to seek out a Latino professor from another department to work with. Through another mentor I came to meet Vivian. Both experiences were a turning point for me. I felt no need to pretend or deny the pain and uncertainty that at times engulfed me. These two wonderful women understood and were able to provide guidance and support my desire to conduct research on Latino/a issues. Having them as mentors encourages me to mentor my Hispanic students to continue on to higher education and positions of leadership in universities. We need to do a better job of recruiting diverse students into education and encouraging them to continue on to higher education and positions of leadership within universities. Having a diverse faculty does make a difference at all levels.

As I begin this new journey as a faculty member, and the only Latina in my department, I at times feel an overwhelming burden, and I find myself besieged by questions. In my courses I am compelled to address issues of diversity, especially with regard to Latino/a students. If I am the "only one," how much care must I take to ensure that my students see this as a relevant issue and not "my issue"? I feel that I should/must be aware and part of all issues related to Latino/a students—even if they aren't necessarily my area. How thin can I be spread? I am warned to guard my time since as a Latina I will be much sought after to participate in various committees throughout the college and university.

How do I balance the need to "represent" with my survival as a tenure-earning faculty member? I have experienced wonderful mentoring relationships with members from the majority culture. Yet, I need that connection with individuals who are culturally and linguistically diverse. How can I call on those individuals while not adding to their already overburdened load?

The Status of Diverse Faculty

The voices of faculty from diverse backgrounds are increasingly being heard across the country. Examples of these voices can be found in two journals: *Black Issues in Higher Education* and *The Hispanic Outlook in Higher Education.* The numbers of diverse faculty at predominately white universities is still alarmingly small compared to the overall U.S. population growth. The U.S. Census reports that by 2020, the population will be comprised of 63 percent Whites, 17 percent Hispanics, 13 percent African American, 6 percent Asian and 1 percent Native American. Ethnic minorities represent approximately 13.8 percent% of the total faculty nationwide. Nonetheless, we have made significant strides over the past twenty years in increasing our representation on university campuses nationally. The percent of change in diverse faculty from 1979 to 2000 is significant in all groups. Especially important is the growth of women faculty from minority backgrounds. For example, for Hispanic women the change was 260 percent and for Asian American women the change was 312 percent. Women are leading their male counterparts in membership in the academy. The absolute numbers, however, are still low. In 2000, 5 percent of the faculty were African American, 2.9 percent were Hispanic, 6 percent were Asian American, and .04 percent were American Indian (U.S. Equal Opportunity Commission, 1983). In contrast to the general population, Hispanic and African American faculty are generally underrepresented at universities.

Additionally, minority faculty is not evenly distributed across institutional types, disciplines or academic ranks. Diverse faculty can choose various institutional settings including community colleges, liberal arts colleges, research universities, women's colleges, minority-serving institutions (e.g., historically black colleges and universities, tribally controlled colleges and hispanic-serving institutions), and most recently, proprietary for-profit institutions (e.g., Phoenix). Minority faculty remain clustered in minority-serving institutions and two-year colleges (Moody, 2004). Furthermore, the differences in gender across different types of universities are striking.

Although data on the numbers of diverse special education faculty are not readily available, one indicator that may help shed light on the issue is the number of doctoral degrees conferred in special education. In 2000-2001, the percentage of doctoral degrees conferred in special education is very low for Black, Hispanic, Asian and Native Americans. The majority of doctorates are conferred to women. Hispanic and African American women were more likely than their male counterparts to earn doctorates in special education (U.S. Department of Education, National Center for Education Statistics, Integrated Postsecondary Education Data System, 1985-1999).

The recruitment and retention of minority doctoral students is important and has been addressed by several authors (Cole & Barber, 2003; Dooley, 2003; Gay, 2004). Of some concern is the fact that only one-third of special education doctoral recipients enter the professoriate (Smith, Pion, Tyler & Gilmore, 2003). Given these statistics, the future pool of candidates for faculty and leaders from culturally and linguistically diverse backgrounds is not promising. The status of diverse faculty in special education is similar to the overall status of minority faculty in higher education. There is much work to be done in increasing the numbers and in convincing administrators at the university that there is great value in diversifying the faculty.

Rationale for Diversifying Faculty: Beyond Equity

The rationale for recruiting and retaining diverse faculty has moved beyond the issues of equal opportunity, affirmative action and equity. Today, one of the strongest arguments for recruiting diverse faculty to predominately white universities and other minority institutions is to ensure a better education for all students and access to diverse scholarly perspectives. "A diverse faculty gives students the opportunity to learn from individuals who differ from them, fosters mutual respect and teamwork, and helps students to communicate effectively with people of varied backgrounds" (Tatum, 2002, p. 2). A diverse faculty can provide a wider range of views and experiences in the courses and curriculum offered at a university.

Many universities have recruitment and retention action plans in place. They point out that quality of life factors and campus/community climate are critical components to successful recruitment of diverse faculty. Diverse faculty can find ways to enhance their quality of life by creating positive work and so-

cial environments on campus. What are the key components for success of minority faculty at universities?

Strategies for Succeeding at Universities

The world of academia can be an exciting and rewarding place to work. However, the research on minority faculty indicates that challenges and barriers to
success are evident (Aguirre, 2000; Cooper & Stevens, 2002; Garcia, 2000a;
Padilla & Chávez, 1995). Although little has been written about the experiences
of minority faculty in special education, there is a wealth of knowledge about
the successes and challenges faced by minority faculty at universities in general.
Many of the recommendations for navigating an academic career come from
the portraits and biographies of diverse faculty (Padilla & Chávez, 1995; Vargas,
2002; Moody, 2004). Among the many recommendations, two major areas of
guidance emerge for diverse faculty: (a) establishing a strong and extended support network and (b) understanding the rules of the game.

Establishing Support Networks

As compared to majority faculty at predominately white universities, minority
faculty report more isolation and marginalization (Fries-Britt, 2000). To counter
the sense of isolation and belonging, minority faculty need to create a rich network of supports. Both formal and informal support networks are important.

Formal Supports

Several support structures are in place for new faculty in a department or college. Often the department chairperson provides the first source of formal support. It is important to schedule regular meetings with the chair for discussing
your yearly teaching, research and service assignments.

Many universities also implement formal mentoring programs for new faculty. Minority faculty are encouraged to use this form of support. Often the
mentor will be a majority senior faculty member who can provide valuable information on how to navigate the first years of your career and help you understand the politics and culture of the institution. When there is a good match
between the mentor and the faculty member, the outcomes for both partners
can be positive. Female new faculty may want to seek out, if possible, a minority

female mentor to assist not only in gaining an understanding of the specific challenges of minority faculty members, but women in higher education.

Minority faculty are often encouraged to connect and build networks of support through university-wide professional development programs. Faculty should take advantage of the services provided by teaching centers and workshops on tenure and promotion, grant writing, cultural diversity and sexual harassment. Support programs such as these also provide an opportunity for diverse faculty to make connections with other diverse faculty on campus. Diverse faculty can also get involved in minority faculty, staff and student organizations on campus. Many universities have well-established associations for Black, Hispanic, Native American and Asian faculty. These associations can connect new faculty to the campus community and provide excellent visibility and support for leadership development.

Informal Supports

Informal sources of support can play a critical role in mediating the stressors and challenges diverse faculty may face at predominately white universities. Usually, the first lines of support come from family and friends. Balancing the academic demands with family obligations is particularly important for women. Many diverse faculty report a tension between work and home (Moody, 2004). Workaholism can be a destructive force in the life of faculty. Yet, faculty are often rewarded for overload. Rendón (2000) realized that the imbalance in her life was inauthentic and took steps to change her life in order to be more authentic, spiritual, loving and caring. She outlines a list of how diverse faculty can be more authentic:

- Find some quiet time during the day for meditation and self-reflection. Honor this time for self-renewal.
- Part of being authentic is taking care of you—saying "no." Understand that by saying "no" you are not rejecting people or devaluing their request.
- Do not commit yourself for at least twenty-four hours before you take on another project that will create overload.
- Find other things besides work to satisfy you. Develop the discipline to set aside this important time for your own personal development.
- Don't get caught up in extremes, don't get caught up in ridiculously high standards of excellence.

- Create space with your friends (and family) to challenge/reflect on what you do, to provide honest feedback.
- Share helpful books, diets, exercise techniques, technology, etc. with your friends [and family]. (p. 151-152).

Another important source of informal support comes from other minority faculty at the universities. Minority faculty can regenerate by building an ethnic critical mass and a place to meet away from the stresses and demands of their academic lives. Peer support networks can meet on a regular basis to celebrate accomplishments, share in Friday afternoon "happy hours," review each other's written work and freely express their concerns to a group of individuals who share their experiences (Fries-Britt, 2000).

Diverse faculty can also turn to community and religious organizations for informal support. If spirituality is important in the lives of diverse faculty, they should find ways to nurture it through various outlets. Faculty can also volunteer in the community to help other diverse members of the community. Additionally, sponsoring diverse student organizations can provide informal support for minority faculty and foster a sense of belonging.

Understanding the Rules of the Game

There are several areas which minority faculty need to recognize as important during the first years of their academic careers. These include (a) negotiating a job offer; (b) understanding the tenure and promotion process; (c) focusing their research agendas (d) balancing service with research and teaching (e) establishing a mentoring relationship and (f) serving as mentors *to* diverse students.

Negotiating a job offer

One of the first experiences faculty will encounter is negotiating the job offer. Negotiating your offer involves more than your salary. Diverse faculty may feel uncomfortable negotiating a job offer for various reasons. Faculty may feel that they should be grateful for the opportunity and are intimidated by majority administrators and faculty. Female and minority faculty may feel unsure about how to "play the game" and will not challenge job offers that are less than optimal.

Understanding the tenure and promotion process

Although many universities provide written guidelines and policies for tenure and promotion, it is important for faculty to understand the unwritten rules on tenure and promotion. Caroline Turner (2000) describes it this way: "It was like there was a script, but I was missing a page or I wasn't given a page" (p. 116). Minority faculty members are often put in a position of convincing and persuading their colleagues of their merits. Their research, if related to race or ethnicity, may not be as valued by their White colleagues as other research. They feel the pressure to give up their racial identities and may often be discouraged from studying their own cultures and problems (Boice, 1992). Turner and Myers (1999) found that faculty of color found the tenure process uniquely stressful, reporting that they often had been told they did not fit "the profile" of someone to be promoted.

Focusing their research agendas

Faculty are expected to "hit the street running" when they start their new positions. New faculty who have begun publishing during their doctoral program are often at an advantage when they begin as assistant professors. It is important to expand one's dissertation research and build a research agenda for the first five years as an assistant professor. Diverse faculty should seek out colleagues at their institutions interested in their research topic and begin a line of collaborative research work. Developing and submitting collaborative research grants will ensure extramural funding for the first few years in a faculty position. Protecting time for scholarly work is recommended and many faculty report reserving one day a week for staying at home to write, knowing that service and teaching obligations can often compete with this time.

Balancing service with research and teaching

Diverse faculty is often burdened with extra service assignments. They are asked to represent their group at various committees, councils and task force activities. This work can be very enticing and rewarding. The heavy service assignments experienced by many minority faculty may indeed prepare them for leadership positions across campus.

Minority faculty are often committed to fostering an inclusive environment on their college campuses, but are often not rewarded for this service when it comes to tenure and promotion (Turner, 2000). Junior faculty should be guided on what service is important, and select service assignments that are important to the campus. Faculty who are in tenure-accruing positions should wait to pursue leadership positions until tenure is achieved. Moving into administrative and/or leadership positions prior to tenure can impede the progress toward tenure.

Once the faculty member is tenured, she can reevaluate her service assignments and take on more of a leadership role in the department, college and university. However, it is not uncommon for a tenured associate professor to take on leadership roles that also impede the progress toward promotion to *full* professor.

Post-tenure mentoring from senior faculty and administrators can assist diverse faculty in choosing an administrative career in academe. Underrepresentation of diverse university administrators is evident on many campuses across the United States Universities should focus more resources on recruiting diverse senior faculty into administration.

Serving as a mentor to diverse students

A faculty's research, teaching and service obligations can leave little time for advising students. Diverse faculty are often sought out by minority students for guidance and mentoring. If the number of diverse students is large, balancing your advisement load can be challenging. It is important for minority faculty to discuss the advisement load with the department chair and assure that they will be recognized and given credit for the work. At the same time, diverse faculty may need to limit the number of advisees that they mentor each term. Serving as a role model to minority students, particularly females, can be extremely rewarding and can help to ensure that women of diverse backgrounds will assume positions of leadership in the future.

Summary

The underrepresentation of diverse faculty in the academy is a significant and complex problem facing predominately white universities in this country. Merely recruiting faculty to the university is insufficient in assuring their success once they are on campus. Larger, research universities continue to struggle in increasing the numbers of diverse faculty. The campus climate remains unfriendly and cold to many diverse faculty.

The underrepresentation of minority faculty in special education has often been explained by the undersupply of job candidates with doctorates entering the academy. However, enormous barriers continue to exist in entry and success of diverse faculty into the professorate. Feelings of not belonging and isolation dominate the reasons why doctoral graduates may not pursue a job at a predominately white university.

For diverse faculty to succeed in academe they must establish strong networks of support and learn the rules of the game. JoAnn Moody puts it this way: "If no one has 'told the truth' and clued you in to the crosscurrents and struggles you will probably experience, you are likely to waste psychic energy being bewildered" (2004, p. 135). This chapter has provided some guidance for diverse junior faculty to successfully navigate the process of the academic world. The authors' recommendations are not only based on the literature related to faculty of color in academe, but also on their own reflections as women of color, of their experiences in higher education.

References

Aguirre, A. (2000). *Women and minority faculty in the academic workplace: Recruitment, retention, and academic culture.* San Francisco: Jossey-Bass.

Boice, R. (1992). *The new faculty member: Supporting and fostering professional development.* San Francisco: Jossey-Bass.

Cole, S. & E. Barber (2003). *Increasing faculty diversity: The occupational choices of high-achieving minority students.* Cambridge, MA: Harvard University Press.

Cooper, J. & D. D. Stevens, (2002). *Tenure in the sacred grove: Issues and strategies for women and minority faculty.* Albany: State University of New York Press.

Dooley, E. (2003). Increasing the number of ethnically diverse faculty in special education programs: Issues and initiatives. *Teacher Education and Special Education, 26,* 264-272.

Fries-Britt, S. (2000). Developing support networks and seeking answers to questions. In M. Garcia (Ed.) *Succeeding in an academic career: A guide for faculty of color* (39-56). Westport, CT: Greenwood Press.

Garcia, M. (2000a). *Succeeding in an academic career: A guide for faculty of color* (1-26), Westport, CT: Greenwood Press.

Garcia, M. (2000b). Weighing the options: Where do I want to work? In M. Garcia (Ed.). *Succeeding in an academic career: A guide for faculty of color* (1-26). Westport, CT: Greenwood Press.

Gay, G. (2004). Navigating marginality en route to the professoriate: Graduate students of color learning and living in academia. *International Journal of Qualitative Studies in Education, 17* (2), 265-288.

Moody, J. (2004). *Faculty diversity: Problems and solutions.* New York: RoutledgeFalmer.

National Center for Education Statistics (2001). *Integrated Postsecondary Education Data System* (IPEDS). Washington, DC: Author.

Padilla, R. & R. C. Chávez (1995). *The leaning ivory tower: Latino professors in American universities.* Albany: State University of New York Press.

Rendón, L. (2000). Academics of the heart: Maintaining body, soul and spirit. In M. Garcia (Ed.) *Succeeding in an academic career: A guide for faculty of color* (141-155). Westport, CT: Greenwood Press.

Smith, D. D., G. M Pion,. N. C. Tyler, & R. Gilmore. (2003). Doctoral programs in special education: The nation's supplier. *Teacher Education and Special Education, 26,* 172–181.

Tatum, C. (2002). *The recruitment and retention of a diverse faculty.* Retrieved on April 12, 2004. from http://coh.arizona.edu/COH/facinfo/diversity/diversity.htm

Turner, C. (2000). Defining success: Promotion and tenure—planning for each career stage and beyond. In M. Garcia (Ed.), *Succeeding in an academic career: A guide for faculty of color* (111-140). Westport, CT: Greenwood Press.

Turner, C. & S. M. Myers, (1999). *Bittersweet success: Faculty of color in academe.* Needham Heights, MA: Allyn and Bacon.

U.S. Department of Education, National Center for Education Statistics, Integrated Postsecondary Education Data System (IPEDS). "Fall Staff" Survey, 1985-1999. Washington, D.C.: Author

U.S. Equal Employment Opportunity Commission (1983). "EEO–6 Higher Education Staff Information" Surveys. Washington, D.C: Author.

Vargas, L. (2002). *Women faculty of color in the White classroom.* New York: Peter Lang.

CHAPTER NINE

Keys to Collaboration for Women Leaders

SHARON F. CRAMER

Other chapters in this book describe the ways in which women rise to positions of leadership; chances are, to some extent, those rises were due in part to the collaborative styles which women developed early in their lives. If you watch little boys, you will likely see games of daring and conquest, while you'll see young girls practice inclusion and taking turns. Carol Gilligan's (1982) observation that women arrive at their responsibilities through care and concern, a different path from the one of justice upon which men focus, illustrates that the path to leadership is not identical for men and women. To an extent, what women typically do as girls (e.g., taking turns) is a healthy preparation for becoming a leader.

However, there is no one way to be a leader. If you were to describe three effective women leaders you have observed throughout your career, chances are they would not be identical in their approach to problem solving, interpersonal styles, or self-reflective practices. There is no single solution to the challenges of collaboration. This chapter will describe keys to collaboration, enabling you to collaborate with many different types of people.

Key #1: Realize that when you become a leader, you will need to learn to work with everyone; you may not have the opportunity to select those with whom you will collaborate.

When you earn a leadership position through appointment or election, the number of people with whom you must collaborate increases exponentially. Even if one consciously selects the upper administrators with whom one will work, people can, and will, change when under pressure. The higher up in administration you move, the more likely it becomes that every few years, an administrator with whom you work will leave and be replaced by a new person. There is a constant need to develop, as well as maintain, effective working relationships.

When facing a new constellation of individuals with whom to collaborate, academic leaders find themselves revisiting Tuckman and Jensen's (1977) classic stages for teams: forming, storming, norming, performing and adjourning. These stages have been referenced in many different disciplines such as working teams in general (Napier & Gershenfeld, 1989), in business (Forsyth, 1990), in schools (Abelson & Woodman, 1983) and in collaboration for special educators (Cramer, 1998). How can you maximize your ability to be an effective, collaborative leader at each of these stages? First of all, you must be attentive to all that you do. For a woman leader, the challenges that a quick temper or a deep thinking style pose to the typical person quickly become magnified. Women leaders with a special education background are even more thoroughly scrutinized, because people presume that all special educators share the common characteristics of patience, thoughtfulness and attentiveness.

Key #2: Make sure you have the collaboration basics mastered.

Women in leadership positions need to develop a radar system for detecting when their verbal or non verbal cues are not what they wish them to be. Watch your tone and your body language, know how to ask and answer questions, probe for information and ensure that the people with whom you are collaborating would rate you as a good listener. While these skills are fundamental for all leaders, they are especially important for women administrators. While men can become forceful or powerful when asking difficult questions, women are generally referred to as "too soft" if they cannot contain their emotions when seeking information. Women must know how to negotiate with power in a way that leads to fair, equitable and gender-free decisions. Calm, focused negotiations are skills that must be acquired.

The focus of the remainder of this chapter is to prepare you for those moments in your career when collaboration appears almost impossible either because the person on the other side of the teeter-totter presents challenges far beyond your collaboration experience or because you realize that you need skills you don't have. By helping you to assess your own skills and identifying the types of problem people or situations who can be challenging you, you will be able to make use of the strategies that will enable you to collaborate with a wide variety of people. Collaboration is not "playing nice with others" or even "going along to get along." Collaboration, for the purposes of this chapter is defined as follows:

> Effective collaboration consists of designing and using a sequence of goal-oriented. The responsibility for collaborating can either be the sole responsibility of one individual who seeks to improve a professional relationship, or a joint commitment of two or more people who wish to improve their working relationship. (Cramer, 1998, p. 3).

There are four principles that many consider the heart and soul of collaboration. These four principles form the basis of the collaboration discussion being presented in this chapter.

1. The goal of collaboration is to create a climate of heightened professionalism between professionals or others with whom the collaborators are working, oftentimes with an indirect impact on student outcomes (Idol & West, 1991).
2. Collaboration "should provide a vehicle to facilitate independent problem-solving on the part of participants" (Johnson, Pugach & Devlin, 1990, p. 11).
3. Collaboration, as described by Idol, West and Lloyd (1988) involves teams of people with diverse expertise working interactively to find creative solutions to problems. The outcome may produce solutions that are different, and perhaps more effective, than a solution that any individual team member would produce independently.
4. Lasley, Matczynski and Williams (1992) state that the significant purpose of collaboration is as a means to sublimate vested interests to the broader purpose of a larger agenda. Women leaders need to be mindful of this purpose as they envision solutions that serve the greater good.

These four principles are useful to all people in leadership positions and should serve as a reminder of the positive aspects of collaboration. Using these principles will assist you in implementing a collaborative climate that will help you to improve your own collaboration skills and to develop a successful collaboration network. Moreover, by practicing these principles you will strengthen your commitment to the collaborative process as a way to lead more effectively.

Key #3: Analyze your collaboration strengths and areas for improvement.

How can you evaluate yourself, and your collaborative practices? Why do so? Farmakopoulou (2002) presents three theoretical frameworks for collaboration: social exchange theory, power/resource dependency model and political economic theory. In social exchange theory "the motivation to collaborate is internal to each . . . and relations are formed when members . . . perceive mutual benefits or gains from interacting, although there is not always a symmetry or equality in the exchange. Consequently, it is suggested that the collaborative relationships are characterized by a high degree of cooperation and problem-solving" (p. 50). In the power/resource dependency model, the presumption is that people "seek to manage their environments to reduce dependencies and uncertainties, including those stemming from other organizations. It also assumes that environmental resources are in short supply" (p. 51). Finally, in political economic theory, in which collaborative groups are, as described by Benson (1975, 1982) "theorized as if context-free. Resource dependencies and other inter-organizational relations are then analyzed without regard to the large political and economic structures in which they are embedded" (Benson, 1982, p. 145). Each one of these theoretical models provides a framework for understanding the nature of collaboration.

Kouzes and Posner (2003) offer a self-analytic approach to collaboration by examining leadership practices. They recommend that leaders consider how they do the following: (1) challenge the process (2) inspire a shared vision (3) enable others to act (4) model the way, and (5) encourage the heart. When considered from the point of view of collaboration strengths and weaknesses, these ideas fit well with the concepts advanced by Cramer and Puccio (2004): they encouraged women leaders in higher education to use these five practices to craft their own collaboration and leadership styles. These concepts resonate with the work of the collaboration specialists, as methods for self-examination. As an example, one of these practices is examined in detail below.

Challenge the process. The effective collaborator is not a "go along to get along" person. Neither is the individual one who bursts down doors to make a point. Consider the following situation:

Dean Sampson learns, via an email from Dean Wells, that Dr. Thomas, a department chair, has "crossed the line" with regard to setting up a new method for interdisciplinary program review. Instead of using the "standard method for program review," she has initiated a new approach, and widely distributed it without going through channels. The approach has both critics and supporters: it is considered radical and insensitive by critics, and bold and pragmatic by supporters. The fellow dean wants to know why she "doesn't have her person in line." What is the Dean Sampson to do?

This situation is an opportunity for two different types of collaboration, which "challenge the process."

Type 1: Peer Collaboration

In collaborating with her fellow deans, Dean Sampson can use this situation as a chance to step back and look at the process of program review. Rather than seeing this situation exclusively as a violation of practice, a woman leader can use this as a chance to examine the program review with her peers. As Anderson (2004) points out in her "many faces of collaboration" piece, "providing . . . service and support is key to relationship building, which represents another facet of collaboration. Relationship building . . . helps to build [collaborative] relationships. Conversely, working in isolation . . . [is] detrimental to [collaborative] relationships" (p. 27). By capitalizing on the opportunity afforded her, Dean Sampson can use the situation as a springboard for conversation with her fellow deans. In fact, Dr. Thomas' action may have triggered a dialogue that was long overdue. Peer collaboration (Van Meter & Stevens, 2000) is a specialized topic of study.

Collaborators who capitalize on naturally occurring events to challenge core assumptions offer a different opportunity to their peers. Why take advantage of these moments? Instead of giving up, or giving in, the campus leader who makes use of these moments can make progress. Fullan (1991) describes the delicate balance needed for progress as "Pressure without support leads to resistance and alienation; support without pressure leads to drift or waste of resources" (p. 91).

The use of a challenging situation to develop new collaborative methods and networks can be a way of turning lemons into lemonade. Fleming and Love (2003), in their description of an organization-wide mentoring model, describe how effective leadership and mentoring are not fleeting, but instead are embedded within the organization's structure. Lazenby and Morton (2003) describe the potential of collaboration to transform both curriculum and people, in describing how coteaching a course led to improved outcomes for students, and for both of the instructors. Thus, Dean Sampson can take advantage of the event to "challenge the process."

Type 2: Superordinate/subordinate collaboration

The chance to collaborate in a superordinate/subordinate working relationship raises the immediate question of "crossing the line" with regard to strict separation of responsibilities. However, the situation as described above can be used to motivate, as opposed to devastate, a proactive department chair that is trying to move things along. In their powerful article, Caron and McLaughlin (2002) describe how "key capacity-building elements related to collaboration between general and special education teachers . . . [led to] a culture of shared responsibility, high expectations for all students and a sense of professional community within the schools" (p. 285). This quote relates directly to how a dean can infuse a highly motivated subordinate with the willingness to reform, without defusing the person entirely. Their article illustrates the elements of capacity building that cross between human capital, social capital, physical capital and system/school capacity. If the shared vision identified by Senge (1990), and described as "shared leadership and collaborative decision-making" by Caron and McLaughlin, was utilized by Dean Sampson, then opportunities for distributed leadership, collaborative culture containing trust, and a sense of professional community might emerge. Caron and McLaughlin have identified these three aforementioned characteristics as indicators of schools seen as "beacons of excellence." These characteristics are defined as follows:

- **Distributed leadership:** "As the flow of power and influence, leadership is not confined to certain roles, but is distributed across roles, with different roles having access to different levels and types of power and influence" (Smylie, Conley, & Marks, 2002, 173–174). The use of the campus curriculum committee, jointly approached by the dean and the department chair, might be explored.
- **Collaborative culture, containing trust:** "A necessary element for successful collaborative culture is an atmosphere of interpersonal safety and trust" (DiPardo, 1999, p. 55). A series of discussions with proponents and critics of the bold move might be initiated prior to taking action.

- **Sense of professional community**: Crow, Hausman and Scribner (2002) state, "Strong professional communities are those that foster collaboration among teachers, use constructive dialogue to critically examine individual teacher practices in group settings, commit to and take responsibility for a shared vision, and rely on a shared commitment to student learning to guide their work" (p. 197).

Dean Sampson, keeping the big picture in mind, should avoid the quick response of disciplining a "disobedient" chair, and instead use this opportunity to strengthen her chairs' commitment to proactive behavior. They should relearn the rationale for "going through channels" but at the same time reconnect to their dean and their institution. The way Dean Sampson handles this situation will be a landmark for her administration, and she had best use it to strengthen, not devastate, a well-intentioned but inappropriate action on the part of her department chairperson.

Collaboration can serve many different functions: as a tool to resolve systemic problems such as disjointed service delivery (Dieker, 2001); to improve the effectiveness of early intervention (Dinnebeil & Hale, 1999) and as a way to improve direct services to students with disabilities in general physical education (Horton, Wilson & Gagnon, 2003); collaboration among general education and special education teachers (Koppang, 2004) and collaboration among school professionals serving culturally and linguistically diverse students with exceptionalities (Roache, Shore, Gouleta & de Obaldia Butkevich, 2003). It is a prominent topic in both general and special education journals (Mason, Thormann, O'Connell & Behrmann, 2004) as well as in the field of creativity (Puccio, 1999).

For women leaders, the use of collaboration is a resource at all levels. Kemelgor and Etzkowitz (2001) discuss mentoring and professional relationships among women as important for their professional growth. Like vitamins, which help to ensure health, a form of collaboration is an essential component of the work life and, ideally, working day of each woman leader. This section of the chapter has described some of the more advanced relationships, the next section focuses on what to do in the face of challenges that may threaten one's career.

Key #4: Master collaboration challenges (proposed strategy for addressing a challenge—either one currently taking place in your professional life, or one that has taken place in the past).

Everyone, even those with excellent collaboration skills, realizes that sometimes one's skill set falls short. When one is working with a difficult person or is having problems with a group that is not responding to a request or expectation, in such situations a full cadre of skills is necessary.

When should you consider a focused effort to improve a collaborative relationship whether with a peer, a subordinate or superordinate? You should add to or improve your collaboration skills when:

- Your collaboration relationship is *overtly negative.* You and your target person have areas of disagreement either recent or long-standing that are apparent to people who know you both. These disagreements could take the form of angry words, hostile looks or general inability to work together well. You may find that you are disappointed with the effect the relationship has on you and on your inability to rise above it.

- Your collaboration relationship is *covertly negative.* You may think you are doing a good job of hiding your true feelings from your target person, but chances are that others with whom you work sense a subtle change in you when you work with this individual. You may in fact go out of your way to avoid encounters, possibly leading to allocations of work based not on talent or position, but on your avoidance of this individual.

- Your collaboration relationship has potential that has not yet been fully realized. You and your target person may have a noncontroversial working relationship. You realize you could become better collaborators.

Major stumbling blocks to collaboration include:

1. Communication projects You and your target person have different communication styles or your own communication skills are deficient and need attention.
2. Assertiveness projects You and your target person are locked in a power struggle and/or your own assertiveness skills are deficient and need attention.

3. Values clash project This intermittent problem between you and your target person may emerge only around certain topics or assignments.

4. Different work styles project You and your target person (a subordinate, peer or superordinate) have different (possibly contradictory) work habits/expectations.

5. Clean slate project You may be ready to move on from a difference of opinion that tarnished an otherwise effective working relationship.

6. Getting to know you project You may use this as an opportunity to build an effective working relationship with a new hire, or a peer on campus, with whom your interactions have been limited. Note: "Should I fire/non-renew this person?" is not a collaboration topic, but some of the ideas presented below can be used to address that question.

Key #5: Build collaboration resource networks: electronic and proximal.

Women leaders often face tremendous isolation in the workplace, rarely having peers with whom they can converse. They are, in fact, "one of a kind" on their campus. If the women are leaders who "rose up through the ranks," former peers cautiously converse with them. If they are new to a campus, the situation is even more complicated—people who try to befriend them often have ulterior motives. Gillett-Karam (2001) explains why she chose the title of "professor president". it is a way to stay connected to her intellectual foundations, helping her feel less alone. She maintained an identity grounded in her intellectual discipline. However, connection to a discipline does not necessarily address challenges faced by women leaders to problem solve regarding delicate situations. To end this isolation, invite people to be one-time or regular members of your collaboration resource network (and note that some of the members of your network can be "virtual").

A collaboration resource network can give you people with whom to bounce ideas around. You can draw your network from any of the following groups:

- People with whom you can comfortably discuss complex topics
- People who you are confident will maintain your confidentiality
- People who have earned your respect and whose feedback you would value

- People who know you well enough to give you genuine feedback on approaches you are considering
- People who have known you long enough to help you compare your behavior in this relationship with other situations in your life

Members of a resource network can help you keep perspective on problem situations, and can be cheerleaders when you are not sure whether or not you are making progress.

The idea of a virtual network and electronic connectivity for collaboration is not new. Rutkowski, Vogel, van Genuchten, Bemelsman, and Favier (2002) describe using technology as "more than a technological substitution for face-to-face collaboration . . . [it] bridge[s] cultural and stereotypical gaps, to increase profitable role repartition between participants and to prevent and solve problems" (p. 219). Bonk (2003) discusses how computer-mediated discussions offer new opportunities for interactions for teacher educators. The idea of extending one's network far beyond synchronous and proximal resources provides a method for extending one's reach—both to offer and receive collaborative assistance. This network is particularly useful when local people are over-informed about the situation at hand, and cannot be impartial. Kirschner and Van Bruggen (2004) describe the benefits of learning and understanding in virtual teams as a method for functional collaboration (e.g., sharing documents and communicating) while supporting adult learners with the flexibility which virtual teams provide in time and space.

Collaborative resources are available electronically that are especially helpful for busy people who only have reflective time at odd hours when others are not available. It also sets the foundation for being a role model in the use of technology for essential functions (beyond personal productivity and email).

Ideally, this chapter has opened a door for you, and you are ready to promote collaboration with a new spirit and energy keeping in mind that when collaboration fails, it still in some way entwines us with the very person with whom we are having so much difficulty. You do, however, have the opportunity to use one or more of the keys discussed in this chapter to improve your collaboration approaches and strengthen your leadership abilities. Clenching teeth, shaking head, going for a run or a swim only put off that inevitable contact. Instead, select one of these keys and give it a try before this week is out.

In her fascinating book, *Composing a Life (1989)*, Mary Catherine Bateson (the daughter of Margaret Mead and Gregory Bateson) describes the ways in which five artists used improvisation to craft their own work, and their own lives. She examines the evolution of artistry as an integral part of life, and her observations are very relevant to the integration of collaboration into one's daily work:

> This is a book about life as an improvisatory art, about the ways we combine familiar and unfamiliar components in response to new situations, following an underlying grammar and an evolving aesthetic. . . . A good meal, like a poem or a life, has a certain balance and diversity, a certain coherence and fit. As one learns to cope in the kitchen, one no longer duplicates whole meals, but rather manipulates components and the way they are put together. The improvised meal will be different from the planned meal, and certainly riskier, but rich with the possibility of delicious surprise. Improvisation can be either a last resort or an established way of evoking creativity (Bateson, 1989, 3-4)

Bateson's challenge to herself is comparable to our challenge to us with regard to collaboration. Women leaders of high caliber need to collaborate confidently. We must find a way to work with all people or at times when necessary, without them. We must not be distracted by them and lose our way. Thus we become enabled to move past the challenges of collaboration and become our most capable selves.

References

Abelson, M. A. & R. W. Woodman (1983). Review of research on team effectiveness: Implications for teams in schools. *School Psychology Review, 12*, 125-136.

Anderson, M. A. (2004). The many faces of collaboration. *Multimedia & Internet @ Schools, 11* (2), 27-28.

Bateson, M. C. (1989). *Composing a life*. New York: Grove Press.

Benson, J. K. (1975). The inter-organizational network as a political economy. *Administrative Science Quarterly, 20*, 229-249.

Benson, J. K. (1982). The framework for policy analysis. In D. Rogers & D. Whetten, (Eds) *Inter-organizational co-ordination: Theory, research, and implementation.* 17-29. Ames: Iowa State University Press.

Bonk, C. (2003). I should have known this was coming: Computer-mediated discussions in teacher education. *Journal of Research on Technology in Education, 36*(2), 95-102.

Caron, E. A. & M. J. McLaughlin (2002). Indicators of Beacons of Excellence Schools: What do they tell us about collaborative practices? *Journal of Educational and Psychological Consultation, 13*(4), 285-313.

Cramer, S. F. (1998). *Collaboration: A success strategy for special educators.* Needham Heights, MA: Allyn & Bacon.

Cramer, S. F. & G. Puccio (2004). Challenging self-imposed constraints: Getting outside the box by transforming leadership through creativity. Keynote address at the Annual Conference of New York State Women Leaders in Higher Education joint presentation with the American Council on Education, April, Buffalo, NY.

Crow, G. M., C. S. Hausman & J. P. Scribner (2002). Reshaping the role of the school principal. In J. Murphy (Ed.) *The educational leadership challenge: Redefining leadership for the 21ˢᵗ century* (189-210). Chicago: University of Chicago Press.

Dieker, L. A. (2001). Collaboration as a tool to resolve the issue of disjointed service delivery. *Journal of Educational and Psychological Consultation, 12*(3), 263-269.

Dinnebeil, L. A. & L. Hale (1999). Early intervention program practices that support collaboration. *Topics in Early Childhood Special Education, 19*(4), 225-236.

DiPardo, A. (1999). Teaching *in common: Challenges to joint work in classrooms and schools.* New York: Teachers College Press.

Farmakopoulou, N. (2002). Using an integrated theoretical framework for understanding inter-agency collaboration in the special education field. *European Journal of Special Needs Education, 17*(1), 49-59.

Fleming, J. & M. Love (2003). A systemic change model for leadership, inclusion and mentoring (SLIM). *Early Childhood Education Journal, 31*(1), 53-58.

Forsyth, D. R. (1990). *Group dynamics.* Pacific Grove, CA: Brooks/Cole.

Fullan, M. (1991). *The new meaning of educational change.* New York: Teachers College Press.

Gillett-Karam, R. (2001). Introduction: Community college leadership: Perspective of women as presidents. *Community College Journal of Research & Practice, 25*(3), 167-171.

Gilligan, C. (1982). In *a different voice.* Cambridge, MA: Harvard University Press.

Horton, M. L., S. Wilson & D. Gagnon (2003). Collaboration: A key component for inclusion in general physical education. *Teaching Elementary Physical Education, 14(3),* 13-17.

Idol, L. & J. F. West (1991). Educational collaboration: A catalyst for effective schooling. *Intervention in School and Clinic, 27*(2), 70-78, 125.

Idol, L., J. F. West & S. R. Lloyd (1988). Organizing and implementing specialized reading programs: A collaborative approach involving classroom, remedial and special education teachers. *Remedial and Special Education, 9*(2), 54–61.

Johnson, L. J., M. C. Pugach & S. Devlin (1990). Professional collaboration. *Teaching Exceptional Children, 22,* 9–11.

Kemelgor, C. & H. Etzkowitz (2001). Overcoming isolation: Women's dilemmas in academic science. *Minerva, 39*(2), 153-175.

Kirschner, P. A. & J. Van Bruggen (2004). Learning and understanding in virtual teams. *CyberPsychology & Behavior, 7*(2), 135-140.

Kouzes, J. M. & B. Z. Posner (2002). *The leadership challenge* (3rd ed.). San Francisco: Jossey-Bass.

Koppang, A. (2004). Curriculum mapping: Building collaboration and communication. *Intervention in School and Clinic, 39*(3), 154-162.

Lasley, T. J., T. J. Matczynski & J. A. Williams (1992). Collaborative and noncollaborative partnership structures in teacher education. *Journal of Teacher Education, 43*(4), 257-261.

Lazenby, R. B. & R. C. Morton (2003). Facilitating transformation through collaboration. *Nursing Education Perspectives, 24* (2), 91–93.

Mason, C., M. S. Thormann, M. O'Connell & J. Behrmann (2004). Priority issues reflected in general and special education association journals. *Exceptional Children, 70* (2), 215-230.

Napier, R. W. & M. K. Gershenfeld (1989). *Groups: Theory and experience* (2nd ed.). Dallas: Houghton Mifflin.

Puccio, G. (1999). Teams. Entry in *Encyclopedia of Creativity, Vol. 2*, 639-649. Academic Press. CA: Tarzana.

Roache, M., J. Shore, E. Gouleta & E. de Obaldia Butkevich (2003). An investigation of collaboration among school professionals in serving culturally and linguistically diverse students with exceptionalities. *Bilingual Research Journal, 27*(1), 117-137.

Rutkowski, A. F., D. R. Vogel, M. van Genuchten, T. M. A. Bemelmans & M. Favier (2002). E-collaboration: The reality of virtuality. *IEEE Transactions on Professional Communication, 45*(4), 219-231.

Senge, P. M. (1990). *The Fifth Discipline: The Art & Practice of the Learning Organization.* New York: Doubleday.

Smylie, M. A., S. Conley & H. Marks (2002). Building leadership into the roles of teachers. In J. Murphy (Ed.) *The educational leadership challenge: Redefining leadership for the 21st centur.* (189-210). Chicago: University of Chicago Press.

Tuckman, B. W. & M. A. Jensen (1977). Stages of small group development revisited. *Group & Organizational Studies, 2*(4), 419-427.

Van Meter, P. & R. J. Stevens (2000). The role of theory in the study of peer collaboration. *Journal of Experimental Education, 69*(1), 113-128.

CHAPTER TEN

Prioritizing the Professional and the Personal

WENDY W. MURAWSKI, POKEY STANFORD,
NANCY M. SILEO AND LISA DIEKER

Are "having a life" and having a career mutually exclusive? Can women in leadership roles also have successful lives as mothers, wives, friends, significant others or even pet owners? The difficulty of finding a balance between the professional and personal has caused many a motivated woman to lose sleep and gain exasperation. In fact, a recent study at the University of California Berkeley reported national data indicating that a woman's chances of securing tenure are greatly reduced if she has children (Wilson, 2003). Imagine how this data would look regarding highly coveted leadership roles in institutions of higher education (IHEs). Does this study indicate that women are unable to maintain a successful career with a fulfilling home life, even in the current "enlightened" milieu? Recognizing that this is a common frustration, and not one unique to a few disorganized or unfocused women, but rather the bane of numerous goal-driven, intelligent and even experienced women, a few of us banded together to explore this conundrum.

The authors of this chapter share many characteristics. We are women in higher education; our passion surrounds individuals with special needs. We have doctorates in special education and we all have tenure or are on a tenure track at our various institutions of higher learning. We met at the beginning of our careers, when we were engaged in board positions for our national organization on teacher education in special education; we recognized in one another the need to combine leadership with fun. We enjoyed one another's company and sense of humor. We realize we were also all struggling with how to find the right balance between our personal and professional lives. This quest led us to work together to share what has worked for us, with others experiencing similar challenges.

We have more differences than similarities, although it is these differences that have perhaps resulted in the depth and breadth of the strategies we will share in this chapter. Wendy Murawski is an assistant professor at California State University, Northridge, a large urban university in the Los Angeles area. She has been married to an actor for three years, is devoted to her cat, and is expecting her first child. Pokey Stanford is an assistant professor at William Carey College in Hattiesburg, Mississippi, a small college in which she is one of two professors of special education. Pokey has been married to a minister (who is HIV positive) for thirteen years, and has three daughters under the age of seven. Nancy Sileo is an associate professor at the University of Nevada, Las Vegas. She is a single lesbian mother, who adopted her daughter during her second semester as an assistant professor. Nancy recently earned tenure and promotion; her daughter is now six years old. Lisa Dieker is an associate professor with tenure at the University of Central Florida, having recently moved from her position at the University of Milwaukee, Wisconsin. Lisa has been married for fifteen years, and has a nine-year-old son, who has recently been identified as having Tourette's Syndrome. These different life experiences brought us together as we explored and shared the diverse strategies each of us has used to maintain that precarious balance between life within the university and the lives we have at home.

In discussing our priorities and our various strategies for making this balance successful, we identified a variety of themes. The first theme to be introduced will get at the heart of what frustrates many professional women how to find ways to value family and self and even how to say "no" with grace. Transitioning from the theme of "saying no with grace" is the need occasionally to say "no" with confidence. Thus, we will explore the role of guilt and politics in the lives of women leaders in higher education. In this theme, we will attempt to provide ways for professional women to differentiate what is necessary, what is helpful, and what is merely chaff. Following guilt and politics, we will address the need to determine where time is best spent in order to maximize all activities. Finding opportunities that will count as three-for-one is a key to maintaining personal and professional balance. Another theme designed to help with prioritizing and maintaining sanity addresses finding time and using technology. Both of these are integral to organizing and balancing the rigorous world of academia.

Family and Self

An immediate stress arises when we consider all of the pressures and expectations on faculty. Women in professional settings can often become overwhelmed with the "to-dos" and the daily unstructured tasks of being a faculty member, including setting and following through with goals. In doing so, however, we frequently forget to include goals related to our personal lives—or even joke (halfheartedly) that we "have no life." It is critical that, in our endeavors to balance our professional and personal lives, we recognize the need to value our families and ourselves as much as we do our career ambitions. In fact, the four of us have realized that, by doing so, we are able effectively accomplish our career goals—and less likely to lose our sanity as we do so!

How does this balance occur? Certainly, as professionals, we need to set priorities and work toward making them a reality within the context of our individual situations. As we have already shared, each of us is in a different professional and personal situation and, in fact, these situations will certainly change over time as we advance in rank, add members to our family structure, or change jobs. We have all discovered, however, that finding ways to say "no" to professional obligations is not an easy task, and in fact, takes practice. All too often new faculty members strive to please everyone around them professionally, at the cost of putting their families on the sacrificial altar of tenure and promotion. This is not a sacrifice worth making and the long-term consequences are detrimental. We have identified some helpful tips that we have used to assist us in valuing our families, friends and selves while pursuing tenure and promotion.

Work with Friends

Look for opportunities with colleagues that will allow you to work smarter, not harder. This search may initially take time and ongoing commitment, but the outcome is worth the effort. Finding friends who share similar research and writing interests can prove to be both fun and energizing. Networking with colleagues from different settings is often beneficial for professional work, but also makes conferences more enjoyable. When working with people we enjoy socially, we suggest scheduling a certain amount of time for the actual "work" to be done, followed by scheduling time to go to dinner, have a drink or perhaps even go shoe shopping! Ultimately, the professional work is accomplished, while time was well spent and not the energy-sapping activity it might have been. An added bonus is that working with others often provides the structure and support that working alone does not. In fact, we have found that working with friends makes us more productive than we may have been otherwise.

Seek Support

It is important as we travel this journey that we remember that, while we may like to be referred to as "Superwoman" or "Wonder Woman," those women weren't trying to get tenure! To manage being a superwoman professionally requires that you know your limits and are willing to ask for help when it is needed. We strongly suggest that professional women seek the support of family and friends when they are feeling overwhelmed. Often women in leadership report concerns about asking for help, seeing it as a sign of weakness. We disagree. We believe that asking for help is a sign of strength, not weakness. If you are married or have a partner, talk with them about your needs *before* you are overwhelmed. Seek out support networks like therapy, friendships, families or book clubs and use them. Depending on your available types of support, there are times when others can take up some of the slack in order to make your life more manageable. At the time of this writing, *our* "support" people are getting us tea, doing our laundry, making travel reservations and being "very quiet so Mom can work."

Let Go of the Guilt—Indulge

As we four explored how we managed to balance and prioritize our lives, one theme emerged rather quickly and yet was surprising for us all. We discovered that each of us had finally come to the realization that there were a few "expectations" of a typical woman that we had determined were not on our priority list. For example, out of our own income, together we employ three housecleaners, two gardeners, one student assistant, a fitness trainer and two babysitters. Two of us pay to have our nails done, all of us pay to have our hair done, and none of us feels guilty about our choices. This did not come easily, however. Each of us went through a time of feeling "guilty" for not keeping up with the dishes, the house, our appearance, the laundry, the kids' homework, or the lawn work. We have since determined that our priorities are such that we would prefer to be successful in our careers and have the ability to enjoy time with our families and significant others. Trying to do those other things in addition simply wasn't feasible, so we made the choice to let them go. We have also learned that making time for movies, shopping, reading and friends isn't just a luxury, it is a necessity! Some of the "luxuries" of life are what keep us going through the long hours. Taking time for oneself and one's family is not a choice that has to be mutually exclusive from one's professional aspirations. Doing some self-maintenance activities and realizing when too much really is too much will keep you balanced.

Say "No" with Grace

Saying "no" continues to be one of the most difficult things for professional women in education to do. We are accustomed to making things happen, to having control, and to ensuring that things are done right. Thus, we often believe that activities simply won't go on without us—or worse, will be done incorrectly. One of the first tips we have is to realize that it is ok to let go. It is ok to let others take up the reins, even if they are not perceived as competent, punctual or as creative as you may consider yourself. It is ok to let yourself off the hook if an activity is not done as well as you might have done it, had you been in charge. Finally, it is critical that you determine which tasks you need to be involved in and which tasks can occur without your input. Setting aside time to be with family, to have a "catch-up" day, or even to just take a day off, can be accomplished by determining ahead of time when that needs to occur, and then staying firm with that decision. When others try to set meetings or appointments during that time, you can say, "I'm sorry, but I'm already booked that day"; congratulate yourself later for having said "no" with grace!

Once you have prioritized your own agenda, it is easier to determine which scholarly or non-university-related activities fit within that agenda. For example, if the department chairperson asks for volunteers to join the Search and Screen Committee, it will be less difficult for you to recognize that you do not need to volunteer. If the dean of the college asks if you would like to join a new task force looking at secondary special education, you can gracefully decline by stating that your focus is on early childhood special education. If your child's teacher sends home a letter asking for volunteers for fund-raising efforts, you can contact him and ask what you can do to help that does not entail excess time or that works within your schedule. If your significant other suggests having a home-cooked meal after a busy week of teaching, you can sweetly ask if he'll be cooking, if you'll be ordering out or if you should dress up for dinner. Sharing with others your priorities and limitations makes being able to say "no" with grace a reality and less of a difficult task. (Authors' note: To be fair, we are all continuing to work on our own skills related to saying "no." We do still have the need to be all things to all people, but it's getting easier. There is hope.)

Guilt and Politics

The balancing act

Balancing what is necessary for our careers (i.e., tenure and promotion) with what is not can be somewhat like walking a tightrope wire without a net. As new assistant professors, we wanted to belong, we wanted to do a good job in teaching, scholarship and service, and perhaps most importantly, we wanted to know what we needed to do to earn tenure and promotion. Of course, each of our institutions is different and, as we've all learned, nothing is written in stone. The rules for tenure and promotion often appear to be mere guidelines that can change at will. Among the big three (teaching, scholarship and service), service is often least considered in the tenure and promotion process. Service often constitutes work on university committees, for the college or department, or with the surrounding educational community, although it may vary at different institutions. However, service frequently takes the most commitment, is the most time-consuming, and in many ways can even be a barrier to tenure and promotion (Patit & Tack, 1998).

   University politics have played a key role in all of our lives—whether we willingly admit this or not. These politics often come in the guise of service to the community—in the form of committees, meetings, activities or other time-consuming responsibilities not directly related to teaching or publication. At one time or another we have all been overwhelmed with service obligations. We have tried to balance these obligations with the requisite high-quality teaching and scholarship. While we can often schedule our teaching load and scholarship days according to our needs, we often find that we are at the mercy of others when it comes to service obligations. Thus, our recommendation is to say "yes" to only a limited number of service obligations each year and to closely monitor the time commitment and benefits involved.

How and why to get involved in university politics

University politics can be time-consuming. They can include being actively in-volved in the union, faculty senate or governing body, or various committees. While having a voice in university politics can be admirable, when you begin down the road of academia it is often wise to first get a handle on your own career path prior to venturing into unknown political waters. Some of our more experienced colleagues have suggested to us that an excellent tactic for a new faculty member is to spend one year just listening. Listen to determine what has been done in the past, what the current issues are, who the key players are and what specific "battles" are worth fighting. Spending that time to learn the sys-tem and to determine what areas are worth your time dovetails nicely into de-veloping your own plan for involvement and achievement.

Successful leaders, female or male, develop and maintain priorities. We sug-gest developing a five-year plan related to all three key areas—teaching, scholar-ship and service. While this plan can certainly be revised as needed, it is always important to have goals in mind as you look to each upcoming activity or op-portunity and consider current and future commitments and obligations. Feel-ings of guilt for not doing it all can be more easily alleviated if this five-year plan is shared with the key players in your department, college or university.

Declining with Confidence

Saying "no" isn't easy, and can be especially difficult for women, even in today's society. In addition, saying "no" with grace isn't always effective in the work-place; sometimes a more definitive decline is necessary. Gender inequities still exist in higher education (Bain & Cummings, 2000; Nettles, Perna & Bradburn, 2000). Unfortunately, they may continue long after we have retired from the profession. Although we try not to focus on this issue or allow it to overshadow our actions, each of us has experienced a time when we felt we were considered less equal than our male counterparts. Our personal findings support those found in the literature; simply put, colleagues are more likely to accept a firm "no" from a male colleague than from one of us. Frequently, strong women are often seen as combative and uncooperative when they say "no," while men are just seen as being "busy" (Bauer & Baltes, 2002).

As women, it is important for us to decline with confidence and expect that we will be treated with professional respect in return. Certainly, perceived colle-giality affects annual evaluations, as well as tenure and promotion, so we must ensure that when we say "no" to a variety of requests, our colleagues, department chairs and deans do not view us as noncollegial. It is important to believe in what we are doing and to know that saying "no" is acceptable. Saying "no" to requests from department chairs and college deans can cause stress and guilt. We have learned the necessity of clearly establishing, for ourselves and others, what is important to our careers and to us personally. Each of us has a teaching and research focus area. We have learned, through trial and error, to say "yes" to those commitments that can be tied to our research or teaching. We have learned to say "yes" to those commitments that are of high interest to us, and we have learned (or are continually learning) to say "no" to everything else. It is important to be strong and self-assured in our choices. It is important to take time to consider a request carefully before making a commitment. After careful consideration, and typically given in conjunction with a valid rationale (and even a five-year plan), it is more than acceptable to say "no" confidently without coming across as noncollegial.

Finding a Mentor

In addition, we have each been lucky to participate in some type of mentoring program; in some cases the mentor was through our institution, another institution, or a professional organization. Our mentors have supported and guided us through the murky maze of university politics. They have supported us when we have been over- or underwhelmed by life at a university. They have cautioned us when we have said "yes" too many times, and they cheered us on when we said "no" loudly for the first time. We suggest that all women, regardless of their role in leadership positions, find someone who can mentor them, whether to provide support, an ear for venting or just for that special connection with someone who understands.

Getting the Three-for-One

We have already mentioned the need to manage family and self, as well as university politics. In doing so, we continue to allude to the necessity of prioritization and determining one's focus. Most IHEs have a process of determining tenure and promotion that is frequently focused on the areas of research/ scholarship, teaching and community service. Depending on the institution, research can be qualitative or quantitative and can take many forms. Some universities require applied research, while others accept a variety of scholarly applications and inquiry for this particular area. The dissemination of such scholarly work can also vary. Certainly, peer-reviewed publications are generally desirable, but other publications, presentations or projects can also be of merit. In the area of teaching, some IHEs are keener on student evaluations of teaching than others. Some institutions require faculty to teach heavier course loads (four or five courses), while others may only require one or two courses or may even allow faculty to buy themselves out of teaching through the writing of grants or through other scholarly opportunities. Service requirements are also defined differently at different establishments.

Regardless of how one's institution defines scholarship and productivity, finding methods of combining time-consuming tasks is always advantageous. The "three-for-one" is a technique that successful faculty have managed to perfect. This entails finding opportunities to engage in an activity that will count for multiple areas in the struggle for tenure and promotion. For example, writing a grant in an area of interest allows a faculty member to get credit for (1) writing and obtaining a grant, (2) conducting research and (3) disseminating the results through publications or presentations. Another example involves finding opportunities in every meeting or activity in which one is engaged. Even "boring" or "obligatory" university meetings have the potential for the three-for-one. Connect with colleagues during those meetings and, while getting the credit for "community service," also use the time to (1) network, (2) determine areas of mutual interest for future collaborative efforts and (3) consider how the activity in which you are currently engaged might lead to a publication, presentation or research endeavor.

This chapter is a specific representation of the success of the three-for-one. All four authors of this chapter met through the Teacher Education Division (TED) of the Council for Exceptional Children. This involvement in our professional organization allowed us to obtain national positions on a board ("community service"), as well as to conduct numerous presentations ("scholarship"). One of the primary benefits of attending professional conferences is the networking involved. This networking led to our collaboration, which has resulted in multiple presentations together. Following one of our collaborative presentations (on how we as female faculty manage our lives in order to be productive and successful educators, wives and mothers), we were asked to participate in the writing of this book. Working with colleagues you really like on a personal level, while simultaneously getting the work done that is necessary for retention, promotion and tenure, is a three-for-one that we all highly recommend!

Finding Time and Using Technology

Time management programs and books the world over espouse the same theme repeatedly: while we can't create more time in a day, we do have power over the way we use our time. What we want to present in this section are the things we have learnedthat help us to be successful in our personal and professional lives. Being employed as faculty members in higher education has taught us the value of maximizing our time. The tips we are sharing fall into two categories: organization and technology. Despite our collective knowledge and goals on the topic of time management, we are all hit by those hidden needs for a quick trip to Krispy Kreme, the family emergency or the unexpected opportunities that result in blowing even the most precise schedules completely off-track.

Using organizational strategies to improve time management

Have a mission. Early on in her career, some very wise females asked Lisa to clearly define what she wanted to do related to the field of special education. Lisa found that it was not until she clearly defined her mission that she was able to be more productive and focused. She has since shared this wisdom with us. We discovered that we had similar experiences. For example, early in our careers, we would all take on whatever project came our way. Now, while we are still tempted to go down the wrong path at times, we try to stay true to our written mission statements. We keep copies of our missions in our desks at home and work, as well as on our Personal Data Assistants (PDAs), so that before we accept one more task we can ask ourselves, "Does this truly relate to what I want to do in the field of special education?"

Never say yes without a day in between. As women known to "get the job done," we frequently experienced times in which the phone would ring and someone would want ask us to do some new task. The task may have sounded fun or intriguing, but when we honestly reflected on the task itself we were able to realize we didn't have the time. In addition, we were often not even the "right" person for the job. Now, when that phone call comes, we recommend stopping to do two things. First, we suggest asking the person who is making the request on our time to describe how the task fits with our mission statement. Second, we recommend identifying a significant other as a gatekeeper for many tasks. This gatekeeper may be a spouse, mentor, family member or friend. For example, keep a write-on calendar on your home office wall. Then, use that calendar as a visual to determine what one more trip or large task that month will do to your family vacation, writing goals or scheduled play dates with your children. See if the commitment piggybacks on an already busy month of travel. Try to commit to only one trip a month and mark on the top of a month once a trip has been scheduled. This strategy can also prevent you from ever saying "yes" in your office at work because you always have to check the master calendar at home. Another strategy involves using your PDA to keep travel requirements organized, in addition to having a large dry-erase board at home to organize your writing agenda. When scheduling travel, projects, committees or writing time, review your weekly and monthly agenda with your gatekeepers to determine if you are beginning to overextend yourself and to determine which activities are acceptable to "let go."

As a group, we have also identified other organizational tips we have found helpful in saving time. These are provided in an easy-to-read, time-saving bullet format.

- Take a sabbatical if you get the opportunity. Don't put it off for when you have more time. This is the "more time" you're looking for!
- Hire a student assistant (with your own money if necessary) to help you keep up with filing, vita,and other office tasks.
- Collaborate with others on articles so you are accountable to someone for deadlines. Take turns determining who will be "lead" author and have the most responsibility.
- Never have more than ten emails in your inbox. Set up files to sort your e-mails and set aside time daily to deal with your e-mail and phone. Faculty who are promoted often are those responsive to students or to leaders who ask for volunteers and committee service.
- Use a phone log in your planner or PDA. This allows you to return calls when there is "down time" like waiting in line.
- Never schedule a full day. By keeping a time log, we learned that only about 40 percent of our time is actually "ours." Try to schedule only four hours of tasks in a ten-hour day and you will be much happier. We can now see our accomplishments and we no longer schedule more things than we have time to complete. In addition, realizing how much time was "ours" made us much more open to students stopping in to

ask questions and allowed us to have time for that unexpected lunch with a friend or colleague.

- List how long a project should take. We suggest trying not to have more than three major things to do at work each day. There are days we do not get the list of three done, but getting two of three done feels much better than two of fifteen!

- Keep your office organized. For example, on Friday put away things from the week and set out any important material for the upcoming week.

Using technology to improve time management

We happen to love technology, but certainly recognize that technology can be both a time-saver and a time-waster. The following suggestions are given with the understanding that different people use technology in different ways and with varying degrees of comfort.

- Make a master PowerPoint presentation and manual each year. Use this material for the courses you teach and the in-services you present. By doing this, our PowerPoint and material has gotten better every year. We also use this material as our excuse to say "no" to schools or colleagues who want us to present on a new or less familiar topic. If it is not already in the prepared material, then we either ask them to change their focus to more closely align with what we have as our area of expertise, or we suggest they find someone who is more qualified for the topic than we are.

- Hang out with other people who like technology. We have learned about most of the "toys" that we enjoy using by finding others who like technology and sharing notes.

- Get a PDA and email service that can be synchronized on the web. This allows you to be able to view your calendar wherever you are and to give others (like your children) access to your calendar.

- Carry around a simple thumb- or jump-drive. These inexpensive gadgets act as mini-hard drives and can store far more information than a simple floppy disk. In addition, they easily transport information from computers at home to computers at school and are useful when collaborating with colleagues.

- Take notes or minutes using a keyboard attached to a PDA. This is a more portable way to take notes than lugging a laptop to each meeting and it reduces the time needed to retype notes after lengthy meetings.
- Learn to use a digital camera, Excel spreadsheets, databases, label makers, Endnotes, CD-RW, DVD-RW, Dreamweaver and other tools that make your work easier to transport and/or increase your production. When in doubt, ask the Information Technology experts at your university.

The bottom line for all of us is time. If technological tools or time-saving tips can give us better outcomes in less time, that is a big positive. We have come to the consensus that the real art of leading is the ability to maintain control even when faced with the pile of commitments, paperwork and stress that can take over a woman in academia who is really trying to "have it all."

Conclusion

Being able to prioritize between the personal and professional continues to be a challenge. Each woman in leadership will find her own unique issues, as well as her own unique methods for dealing with those issues. However, we have found that sharing strategies and suggestions with one another has helped us to become stronger in our roles as leaders, colleagues, wives and mothers. The suggestions in this chapter came from our personal experiences, from experiences shared with us by friends and colleagues, and from the literature.

The field of special education is highly demanding, as are leadership roles in IHEs. When combining special education, leadership and the specific challenges that professional women face, it is no wonder that many women struggle to achieve a balance, finding that the combination is simply too overwhelming. We must learn from those who have made it work, who have successfully prioritized and managed the various aspects of their lives. We hope that the suggestions we have offered in this chapter will add to the literature and assist more women to find strategies that help them achieve their own personal and professional goals.

References

Bain, O. & W. Cummings (2000). Academe's glass ceiling: Societal, professional, organizational and institutional barriers to the career advancement of academic women. *Comparative Education Review, 44*(4), 493-514.

Bauer, C. C. & B. B. Baltes (2002). Reducing the effects of gender stereotypes on performance evaluations. *Sex Roles: A Journal of Research, 47*(9-10), 465-476.

Nettles, M. T., L. W. Perna & E. M. Bradburn (2000). Salary, promotion and tenure status of minority and women faculty in US colleges and universities. *Education Statistics Quarterly, 2*(2), 94-96.

Patit, C. L. & M. W. Tack (1998). Women and faculty of color: Higher education's most endangered resources. *National Association of Student Affairs Professionals Journal, 1*(1), 7-25.

Wilson, R. (2003). How babies alter careers for academics. *The Chronicle of Higher Education, 50*(15), A1.

Contributors

Vivian I. Correa is currently the Associate Dean of the Graduate School at the University of Florida and has been a professor in the Department of Special Education since 1985 where she served as department chairperson in 1996-1999. Her Ph.D. is from George Peabody College of Vanderbilt University. In 2000-2001, Dr. Correa served a one-year term as the Matthew J. Guglielmo Endowed Chair at California State University, Los Angeles. Dr. Correa's areas of expertise are in early childhood special education, bilingual special education, collaboration and teaming, culturally responsive intervention and working with families. She has extensive publications in these areas. Dr. Correa has served as the coeditor of *Teacher Education and Special Education* and is currently on the national board of the Council for Exceptional Children. She is a native Puerto Rican and is fluent in both English and Spanish.

Sharon F. Cramer is a professor of Exceptional Education at Buffalo State College in New York. She has served as an officer of several state, regional and national organizations, and most recently as president of the Northeastern Educational Research Association (NERA), a regional affiliate of the American Educational Research Association. The author of numerous publications, Cramer has delivered more than eighty presentations at local, state, national and international conferences, with emphasis on collaboration in the workplace. In 2003, she received the Burton Blatt award from the Division on Developmental Disabilities of the Council for Exceptional Children, recognizing her lifelong commitment to advancing the services of people with disabilities.

Lisa Dieker is an associate professor in the Department of Child, Family and Community Sciences at the University of Central Florida (UCF). She was recently selected for the prestigious position of University of Central Florida Teaching and Learning Academy Fellow. Prior to coming to UCF, Dr.

Dieker served for nine years on the faculty at the University of Wisconsin where she was the codirector of a federal-, state- and foundation-funded project at the University of Wisconsin-Milwaukee/Milwaukee Public Schools. She has written numerous articles in the areas of collaboration, diversity and co-teaching.

Susan Donovan has a degree in Early Intervention/Special Education with a particular interest in family involvement and public policy. She began work in the field of early intervention and special education over twenty-five years ago as a mother and has been a service provider, educator, consultant and supervisor. Her experience includes policy research and development, technical assistance and training in early intervention, children's mental health, mental retardation and autism for children birth to age twenty-one. She provided technical assistance to the U.S. military Early Intervention program overseas and assisted in its implementation. She currently works as a consultant and grant project coordinator and holds a faculty position at the University of Central Florida.

Pamela Gillet has professional experience as a general and special education teacher, transition specialist, special education department chair, special education supervisor, principal, director of special education and superintendent of schools. She has also directed a teacher preparation grant and has taught as an adjunct professor at four universities in the Chicago area. Dr. Gillet has authored three books and numerous journal articles. She has presented activities and offered sessions at international, regional and state conferences. She has been president of the Council for Exceptional Children, the Illinois Council for Exceptional Children, the Illinois Administrators of Special Education and the Yes I Can! Foundation.

Diane Johnson is the Director of the FDLRS/Miccosukee Center located in Tallahassee, Florida. She has been both a general and special education classroom teacher. Diane has served on numerous committees related to the education of students with exceptionalities and the training of school personnel. She has presented at local, state and international conferences. Her leadership roles are many and include serving as president of the Council for Exceptional Children and as president of the Coalition for the Education of Exceptional Students. She received the Landis M. Stetler Award from the Florida Federation Council for Exceptional Children, and is a recipient of the Distinguished Educator Award for Public Schools from the Florida State University College of Education Alumni Association.

Marsha H. Lupi has been an associate professor in the Department of Special Education at Hunter College of CUNY for twenty-seven years. She served as department chairperson for ten years and was also the assistant dean of the School of Education. Dr. Lupi is currently the Children's Action Coordinator for the Teacher Education Division of the Council for Exceptional Children and has served as the president of the New York State CEC unit. She is a recipient of the Distinguished Alumni Award for Outstanding Leadership and Contributions to Special Education, Teachers College and Center for Opportunities and Outcomes for People with Disabilities. Her research and teaching efforts are focused on mentoring women special educators to leadership positions in higher education, current issues in special education and preparing culturally competent special education teachers.

Linda Marsal is the Associate Director of the Council for Exceptional Children. Her career has encompassed nearly every aspect of special education. She has taught exceptional students from every grade level including students with gifts and talents and college courses for both regular and special education. She served in special education administration for twenty-four years as a director of exceptional education, supervisor and principal where she made significant contributions to special education. Since joining CEC in 1966 as a member, she has served in numerous leadership positions at the state, national and division level, including president of the organization. As CEC president she established the Presidential Commission on the Conditions in Special Education, which led to the "Bright Futures Report" in 1999.

Suzanne M. Martin is a professor of Exceptional Education and Assistant Dean of Accreditation and Administration at the University of Central Florida. Dr. Martin has a long history of leadership activities in higher education as well as educational organizations. She currently serves as the President of the Council of Exceptional Children. In her career, Dr. Martin has taught elementary school students, junior high school students with special needs, community college students preparing to be paraprofessional in special education classrooms, undergraduate students and graduate students. She has been awarded grants from the U. S. Department of Education that have allowed her to pursue her work in teacher education. She is the recipient of many awards and the author of numerous articles on teaching and leadership.

Patricia Alvarez McHatton is an assistant professor at the University of South Florida in the Department of Special Education. She received her Ph.D. at the University of South Florida in Special Education Curriculum and Instruction with an emphasis in urban education. She is a National Board certified teacher and a Professionally Recognized Special Educator. Dr. McHatton was a recipient of the 2004 Outstanding Dissertation Award from the University of South Florida. Dr. McHatton is a native of Cuba. Her research interests include the education and empowerment of culturally and linguistically diverse students through participatory action research and issues of stigma and discrimination for culturally and linguistically diverse families and students.

Kathleen McSorley has been the assistant dean for teacher preparation programs and NCATE coordinator for the initial accreditation of Brooklyn College for nearly three years. She is an assistant professor of special education, and headed the graduate program in special education for six years. Her scholarship interests include creating optimal learning environments for students with emotional and behavioral issues, teacher preparation, the preparation of administrators for inclusive schools and classrooms and creating learning organizations that lead to systemic change. She was a special education teacher and staff developer in the New York City Public Schools for twenty-three years.

Wendy W. Murawski is an assistant professor in the Department of Special Education at California State University, Northridge, where she chairs the Mild-Moderate Disabilities specialization. She is in her second elected term as secretary on the executive board to the Teacher Education division of the Council for Exceptional Children. In addition, Dr. Murawski is Director of Research for the CHIME Institute, an organization supporting the full inclusion of students with special needs. A national presenter with the Bureau of Education and Research, she travels frequently to provide workshops and consult on co-teaching and inclusion. Her research and publication interests are in co-teaching, collaboration and teacher preparation.

Nancy D. Safer has more than thirty years of experience in special education, and currently works as a managing research scientist at the American Institute for Research. Dr. Safer is the former executive director of the Council for Exceptional Children where she provided, for almost ten years, strategic and operational leadership in the management and coordination of the organization of more than 50,000 special educators, related professionals and families. Prior to moving to CEC, she worked for seventeen years in various positions at the U.S. Department of Education, Office of Special Education Program. She began her special education career as a special education teacher in the Philadelphia Public Schools.

Mary Senne completed a master's degree in psychology in 1984 and worked in the mental health field for ten years in public and private settings. She completed her Ph.D. in Exceptional Education from the University of Central Florida in May of 2005. In 1992, she began working in the disability community in central Florida. Efforts included development of a behavioral center for children with a diagnosis of autism, followed by the creation of a Center for Autism and Related Disabilities (CARD). Mary founded the Jennings Exceptional Education Institute in 1998 at the University of Central Florida with the goal of better preparing teachers to work with families of children with disabilities. Mary is married with three children, one of whom is autistic.

Deborah A. Shanley is the Dean of the School of Education at Brooklyn College of the City University of New York. Previously, she served as Dean of the School of Liberal Arts and Education and was a faculty member and Director of the Special Education Program at Medgar Evers College for more than fifteen years. Over the years, Dr. Shanley served in the role of President of NYS CEC, NYS Association of Behavior Analysis and the Berkshire Association of Behavior Analysis. She is actively involved with the National Network for Educational Renewal and serves on its Governing Board. In March 2004, she was elected the Chairperson of the Council of Great City Colleges of Education Committee within the Council of Great City Schools and serves on its executive committee.

Nancy M. Sileo is an associate professor of early childhood special education and early childhood education at the University of Nevada Las Vegas. Dr. Sileo has worked in the field of ECSE/ECE for more than fourteen years. She is active in a number of professional organizations including CEC, DEC and TED. Nancy has served on the TED Board via the Conference Advisory Committee for ten years—first as a student member, then as a professional member and finally as the chair of the committee. Her current interests include infancy, HIV/AIDS prevention education, teacher education and ethical issues in teacher education.

Barbara P. Sirvis is President of Southern Vermont College, a small, independent, career-oriented liberal arts college in Bennington, Vermont. Prior to her current position, she held increasingly responsible administrative positions at different institutions. She held faculty appointments in special education at the University of Washington and San Francisco State University. She began her career as a classroom teacher of students with physical and multiple disabilities. Dr. Sirvis has served in professional leadership roles in the Council for Exceptional Children including Governor-at-Large on the CEC Executive Committee. She also served as a member of the National Board for Professional Teaching Standards Subcommittee on Special Education Standards. Dr. Sirvis received her doctorate from Teachers College, Columbia University, and completed the Management Development Program and Seminar for New Presidents at Harvard University.

Pokey Stanford is an assistant professor of education at William Carey College. Dr. Stanford was a classroom teacher for seven years prior to coming to the university level. She is active in professional organizations, including serving as the newsletter editor for the Teacher Education Division of the Council for Exceptional Children. She is the mother of three children, Sarai Grace, Juli Anna and Emma Leigh, and has been married to Shane Stanford for the past fourteen years. Her current interests include MI theory and Technology as intervention tools to further facilitate inclusive environments for all learners.

Lee Ann Truesdell is associate professor of special education at Queens College, City University of New York. Specializing in the areas of learning disabilities, inclusion and qualitative research methodology, she teaches courses in curriculum, consultation and collaboration, and research. Funded by OSERS, she directed a five-year grant for the recruitment and preparation of underrepresented groups for special education teaching in inclusive and culturally diverse settings. For the past five years she served as assistant and then associate dean of education. As assistant dean, she facilitated the re-registration of all programs leading to teacher certification by working with faculty to redesign programs to meet new state regulations for teaching. Most recently, she led the College's preparations for initial NCATE accreditation.

Jane M. Williams was on the faculty of the University of Nevada, Las Vegas, College of Education until May 2005, when she accepted a position at Towson State University in Maryland. Dr. Williams worked with the Office of Special Education Programs, U.S. Department of Education, for five years. During those years, she served as an Education Program Specialist— Expert, Transition in the Monitoring and State Improvement Division and as the Associate Division Director for Secondary, Transition and Postsecondary Programs in the Research to Practice Division. Prior to joining the

U.S. Department of Education, Dr. Williams held various teaching and administrative experiences in public schools for nineteen years in four states. In these positions, Dr. Williams worked with students with and without disabilities in first through twelfth grades.

Studies in the Postmodern Theory of Education

General Editors
Joe L. Kincheloe & Shirley R. Steinberg

Counterpoints publishes the most compelling and imaginative books being written in education today. Grounded on the theoretical advances in criticalism, feminism, and postmodernism in the last two decades of the twentieth century, Counterpoints engages the meaning of these innovations in various forms of educational expression. Committed to the proposition that theoretical literature should be accessible to a variety of audiences, the series insists that its authors avoid esoteric and jargonistic languages that transform educational scholarship into an elite discourse for the initiated. Scholarly work matters only to the degree it affects consciousness and practice at multiple sites. Counterpoints' editorial policy is based on these principles and the ability of scholars to break new ground, to open new conversations, to go where educators have never gone before.

For additional information about this series or for the submission of manuscripts, please contact:

Joe L. Kincheloe & Shirley R. Steinberg
c/o Peter Lang Publishing, Inc.
275 Seventh Avenue, 28th floor
New York, New York 10001

To order other books in this series, please contact our Customer Service Department:

(800) 770-LANG (within the U.S.)
(212) 647-7706 (outside the U.S.)
(212) 647-7707 FAX

Or browse online by series:

www.peterlangusa.com